Queer Theory and *Brokeback Mountain*

FILM THEORY IN PRACTICE

Series Editor: Todd McGowan

Editorial Board

Queer Theory and *Brokeback Mountain*

MATTHEW TINKCOM

Bloomsbury Academic
An imprint of Bloomsbury Publishing Inc

B L O O M S B U R Y
NEW YORK • LONDON • OXFORD • NEW DELHI • SYDNEY

Bloomsbury Academic

An imprint of Bloomsbury Publishing Inc

1385 Broadway	50 Bedford Square
New York	London
NY 10018	WC1B 3DP
USA	UK

www.bloomsbury.com

BLOOMSBURY and the Diana logo are trademarks of Bloomsbury Publishing Plc

First published 2017

© Matthew Tinkcom, 2017

All rights reserved. No part of this publication may be reproduced or transmitted in any form or by any means, electronic or mechanical, including photocopying, recording, or any information storage or retrieval system, without prior permission in writing from the publishers.

No responsibility for loss caused to any individual or organization acting on or refraining from action as a result of the material in this publication can be accepted by Bloomsbury or the author.

Library of Congress Cataloging-in-Publication Data
A catalog record for this book is available from the Library of Congress.

ISBN: HB: 978-1-5013-1881-8
PB: 978-1-5013-1882-5
ePDF: 978-1-5013-1884-9
ePub: 978-1-5013-1883-2

Series: Film Theory in Practice

Cover design: Alice Marwick
Cover image: Eve Sedgwick, photo courtesy of H. A. Sedgwick (Top) / still from Brokeback Mountain (2005) © FOCUS FEATURES / THE KOBAL COLLECTION (Bottom)

Typeset by Deanta Global Publishing Services, Chennai, India
Printed and bound in the United States of America

For Stephen Link

CONTENTS

ACKNOWLEDGMENTS

Todd McGowan asked me to think about the topic of queer theory and how one might explain it through one film. The challenge of deciding upon that film and of doing so has been exciting, and I thank him for the opportunity and for his support throughout the writing process. All virtues in this book accrue to his insights, while all shortcomings are mine.

The editors at Bloomsbury have been immensely patient in the writing and editing process and I thank them.

Stephen Link listened to me talk about this project more than any patient soul would need to and gave me his wisdom, questions, humor, and love. For that, and for everything, I am always grateful. Stewart Waller, Al Hoff, Timothy Credle, and Tilly Carpenter each gave friendship and support as I wrote. Gary Ross kindly supplied me with coffee.

Georgetown University provided a research grant for the completion of this project and it confirms my happiness in calling The Hilltop my home.

PREFACE

I was raised in my early childhood life in the American west and, as a queer boy, soon became attuned to the forms of masculinity that the cowboy aesthetic made present to me. My father's family ranched in Colorado and my earliest memories are of the Rocky Mountains and ranching life as a backdrop to daily life, as well as memories of the men who formed the social life of ranching, rodeos, and cowboy culture. I was also, having been born in the early 1960s, aware of the tension brought about by the hypermasculinity of the place: it seemed in the terms that queer theory scholar Eve Kosofsky Sedgwick later offered me, both homosocial and homosexual—the latter part, at least forming a part of my nascent sexuality.

Later in my young adult life I lived on a ranch in California, where I also attended college. Working on the ranch in Deep Springs College in the Inyo White mountains that straddled the border between California and Nevada, I became even more aware of how much the western ideals of cowboy life resonated with the seemingly contradictory fact of the intense bonds of social intimacy and physical proximity among men that seemed to proscribe any mention of the erotic aesthetic of the cowboy life. When later in graduate school in the mid-1980s I discovered Sedgwick's book, *Between Men*, I was animated by her insights into how that contradiction operates; despite the fact that that book examined English literature of the nineteenth century, it articulated a phenomenon to which I had often born witness.

I mentioned this fact to Eve Sedgwick when I met her in the early 1990s and she offered an astonishing fact: she had by dint of her marriage to an alumnus of Deep Springs come to know about the place and she revealed how Deep Springs informed the writing of *Between Men*. I do not recall much about the details of that conversation aside from my astonishment about the connection, but when I first encountered *Brokeback Mountain* in reading Annie Proulx's short story in *The New Yorker* magazine, I wondered about whether the two male protagonists could ever be related in critical fashion. The subsequent production of the film that was adapted from Proulx's fiction continued to press this connection and I still regret that I was unable to have the opportunity to ask Eve about her thoughts on the film. Her death in 2009 still makes me sorry about that.

However, Gary Needham's book on the film, *Brokeback Mountain*, set into motion my sense that the film's importance for understanding the state of queer politics and queer theory should not be underestimated, and this book in many ways is in conversation with the ideas contained within Needham's book. If the two were to sit side by side on the reader's shelf, that would make me happy. From Needham's account we should learn that the film is anomalous in the odd position it inhabits in contemporary cinema and poses residual questions about how to interpret it: Is it a Hollywood film that sets new agendas and possibilities for the film industry? Is it, according to the terms Needham sets forth, an independent "niche" film whose production seems at odds with the guiding interests and values of the corporate film industry, one whose appearance should not be taken to augur much of a commitment by the US corporate film industry to telling stories about queer people's lives?

The present account takes a highly personal turn in that we live historically and cannot know what long-term effects the film might have. I here offer to the reader who may not have previously engaged in the practice of queer theory the opportunity to learn about some of the stakes of reading through the lens of queer theory. One of the immense virtues of Ang Lee's film is that it offers us the chance to see the complexities and ambiguities of queer life: one viewer will take away the memory of the vital bond between Ennis del

Mar and Jack Twist, while another will see it as another installment in the grim outcomes of queer sexuality within homophobic culture. However, before we might decide upon any such reading—or, if that is even possible—we shall discern in the following pages the powerful philosophical and analytical tools that some of the central figures of queer theory offer to us.

Matthew Tinkcom,
August 2016

Introduction

Brokeback Mountain tells a deceptively simple story of the intimate emotional and sexual bonds between two men, Ennis del Mar and Jack Twist. Set in the mid-twentieth-century American western states of Wyoming and Texas and spanning the decades from the 1960s to the 1980s, the film depicts Ennis and Jack's meeting as sheepherders and the first summer they spend on the film's eponymous mountain, where they grow close, have a sexual relation, as well as come to have great affection for each other. They part at the end of the summer of 1963 and do not see each other for four years. By the time they meet again, they are both married and have had children, but the relation between them is reanimated and over the course of many years they reunite each summer in the Wyoming mountains, all the while staying in their respective homes and lives, Ennis in Wyoming and Jack in Texas.

Their marriages each change; Ennis divorces his wife Alma, while Jack works in his wife Lureen's family business, but they never lose a hold on each other, and that fact troubles them both. Jack Twist hopes for more fully shared life between him and Ennis del Mar, proposing on several occasions to Ennis that they could live and ranch together and expand the bond between them. This never comes to pass, and Ennis comes to learn that Jack has died in Texas under circumstances that are not entirely made clear within the film. The story concludes with Ennis living alone in a remote part of Wyoming with a few small tokens that bear the memory of Jack Twist for him.

Directed by the Taiwanese-American director Ang Lee and released in 2005, the film was based on a short story of the same name by Annie Proulx, which was first published in *The New Yorker* magazine in October of 1997 and subsequently in short novel form the following year. Proulx's fiction was adapted for Lee's film by Diana Ossana and Larry McMurtry, the latter figure having established himself as a prominent writer of novels and screenplays about the western United States. The film was nominated for multiple awards, most prominently for eight categories in the Academy of Motion Pictures Arts and Sciences annual Oscar awards, and won in three categories there: Best Director for Lee, Best Adapted Screenplay for Ossana and McMurtry, and Best Original Score for composer Gustavo Santaolalla.

These bare facts about *Brokeback Mountain* only begin to suggest the importance of the film for the history of cinema because the film set in motion a wide discussion about its depiction of two white rural uneducated working-class men having a sexual and romantic bond. Even prior to its release, the film was quickly named in shorthand fashion by the popular press as "the gay cowboy" movie, and much of the ensuing popular and critical response to the film saw this controversial naming as heralding a significant change in the way that the American film industry could handle stories about same-sex sexual relations and made one wonder whether such films might garner appeal among Hollywood audiences.

"The gay cowboy" movie as a way of describing *Brokeback Mountain* is ironic because Ennis and Jack herd sheep, do menial labor, and sell tractors, hardly the work of the iconic cowboy of the American west. Nor are they gay in the way that we use that term as a legacy of the past four decades of the struggles by gay men, lesbians, bisexual people, and transgender people in the United States and around the world for full inclusion in the political protections offered by the law and for social participation more generally. These vital activities have altered human societies irreversibly and for the better, but they are part of a world that would have been unrecognizable to Ennis and Jack.

The only term that the two men ever use in the film (and in Proulx's short story) to possibly describe their bond is that of *queer*, and they do so in order to disavow it. The strong derision that they both express toward the name ("I'm not no queer" remarks Ennis—"me neither" responds Jack) discloses to us the threat of violence and rejection that has historically been conveyed by calling someone "queer," a threat so serious that neither man can do anything but reject it. Before there were any of the positive and affirming names of gay, lesbian, bisexual, trans and the like, queer was a name for same-sex sexuality that had to be resolutely loathed. It is no wonder that Jack and Ennis seek to evade it, even as it approximates what they are experiencing: they are not queer solely because of the sexual relation between them, but queer in the idea that that the relation fosters within them ideas, responses, behavior, emotions. and language that neither knows how to live with. Be that as it may, the shorthand nomination of the film as "the gay cowboy" movie stuck and, despite its less-than-accurate description, it took hold of the popular imagination about the film. Admittedly, the film's ultimate popular epithet "the queer sheep-herder" hardly justifies the allure that the film has come to have.

With this in mind, this book is intended to serve as an introduction for the reader to a body of critical knowledge called queer theory and to offer insight into *Brokeback Mountain*. The reader is assumed to come to the project with a little advance reading or instruction in the area of queer theory or within film studies, and the sole preparation needed to learn from this book is an interest in understanding how the more general concepts of queer theory have established important ideas that have organized discussions in the past thirty years in fields as various as philosophy, sociology, anthropology, law, sex/gender studies, media studies, and literary studies, to name a few.

It should be clear at the outset that the book is meant to guide the reader through central concepts within queer theory, but equally clear should be the fact that the intellectual work and activism of queer theory is now so deeply entrenched in scholarly and public spheres that no volume could encompass all of the activities that are included in queer theory. Indeed, a testament to the power of the ideas contained within the field is the prevailing sense that it has redefined how contemporary men and women think about and live their sexuality, their gender, and the modes of identity politics that are informed by those aspects of their lives.

Queer theory can hardly be exaggerated in terms of how the various ideas it has introduced to contemporary thought have reshaped the discussions that we have about the relation of our sexuality to our lives; from HIV/AIDS activism to marriage equality, from discussions about disparities of power between men and women to the politics of trans subjects, from violence aimed at LGBQT individuals to the new media landscape that grapples with a public culture of queers in fictional and nonfiction representations, all of these matters bear a relation to the work of intellectuals working in the broad field of queer theory.

That said, the idea that queer theory itself is a field should immediately raise questions, given that there are few actual institutional homes where queer theorists are self-identified within their fields, and, paradoxically, it may turn out to be that part of the powerful transformative effect of queer theory has been that it is not—at least, not *yet*—located within very many colleges, schools, departments, programs, or research institutes that bear the name of queer theory or queer studies. On the academic side of queer theory, were one to go looking in a college or university for the people working within the domain, one would find thinkers, writers, and researchers in English, philosophy, sociology, or film departments, or in medical, law, or public policy schools. Likewise, if one were seeking queer theorists engaged in activism and the shaping of public discourses and related regulatory activities, one would discover them in issue-focused organizations that seek to work on the manner in which sexuality and gender are moral and legal nodes within a broad network of actors seeking social justice.

The discovery of how dispersed and simultaneously widespread practitioners of queer theory are signals to us the fact that the many figures associated with the field develop their interest in a variety of intellectual and scholarly traditions even as they share queer theory's central and organizing concerns. It also tells us that queer theory has been, since the name first emerged in the early 1990s, interdisciplinary because its concerns have been with the fact of exclusion, domination, and silencing of as well as the violence meted out to LGBQT people, and every tool that might help to alleviate those negative effects of heteronormative thinking has been needed.

In this regard, queer theory is not a discrete field concerned with maintaining boundaries around appropriate topics and manners of producing knowledge about them as might be discovered in more traditional academic fields; instead, it has happily borrowed the intellectual practices that might serve it in the interest of intellectual, personal, and social reinvention in the face of systemic exclusion and violence toward queer people.

The very name of the field—*queer* theory—when it appeared for the first time in the 1990s was intended to challenge powerful forms of naming through hate speech: the term "queer" as mentioned above has a long history as an epithet used to threaten, silence, and discipline those individuals and their communities who were seen as non-conciliatory to expected forms of social behavior and assumedly (but not always) related kinds of sexual behavior. By taking on the very same name which was to be avoided at all cost, the early thinkers of queer theory sought to drain from the word its toxic and harmful intent.

Additionally, a motivating idea was that the theory itself needed to be "queer": unexpected, unpredictable, antagonistic, and capable of producing uncomfortable insights into the techniques through which lesbians, bisexual people, gay men, and trans people have often had their lives defined by terms not of their making. One of the primary motivations for queer theory has been to ask "truth to power" and to make those people—including many LGBQT individuals—ask themselves how they participate, consciously or inadvertently, in techniques of violence, domination, and control.

Queer theory can thus be understood as asking questions that are historical and questions that are philosophical, and the two modes of questioning are interrelated and inform each other. Broadly speaking, the historical questions posed by queer theory ask about how systems of gendered normativity and control in the past have shaped the ideas and assumptions of the present era in ways that we might not even be aware of, and also how human societies in other prior eras and other places might have thought very differently about sexuality and gender to a degree that we could well be challenged to make sense of these ideas as they relate to our own.

This leads to one of the primary insights which queer theory offers: that human sexuality and gender are highly varied over time and place and that, as is discussed below, biological sex might seem to be a universal human phenomenon, but the meanings attached to such biological functioning differ immensely, even within a particular society that might initially seem to be highly cohesive and consistent in its modes of thought and practices about gender and sexuality.

The questions of queer theory

Queer theory should most effectively be understood as a conjoined set of questions about the roles that gender and sexuality play in human societies, both in the past and in the present. These questions conjoin both our intellectual capacity to make sense of the human social world and our capacity to labor as men and women to transform those social practices that have engendered the harm done toward LGBQT people as a matter of course. Thus, queer theory carries with it a set of questions that seek to understand, theoretically and historically, the bases on which nonnormative genders, sexual aims, and sexual pleasures are situated within relations of power and are therefore already political relations, whether they might seem so or not. Further, LGBQT activism finds its endeavors by engaging such histories and theories in order to seek out those political projects that can alter the practices and institutions which marginalize, harm, or neglect LGBQT people.

What are these animating questions of queer theory, then? We can organize them into three categories, each of which is interrelated with the others:

1. *Historical*: How did humans in prior eras think about sexuality and gender? Were those things even meaningful categories to them—did they even think and live in regard to such terms? Did they have similar or highly dissimilar ways of understanding how what we think about sexuality and gender identity organizes our lives? If not, what categories and explanations were available to them? Did such categories include everyone within a given society, or were particular figures—often, for example, men—privileged while others were denied inclusion? How did those societies explain these ways of thinking about sexuality or gender and were they aware of the implications of thinking in such ways? Do we bear the legacy of these ways of thinking? That is, have we inherited some of these ideas and models and do we practice them—even unawares—in the present era?

One historian of ideas who addressed these questions with surprising results was Michel Foucault. Foucault examined the meanings and values that different societies have attached to sexuality, and he aimed to demonstrate through his historical research how such meanings and values were highly changeable and have varied among historical eras. Foucault's research began with more contemporary moments—the nineteenth century to the present—but his subsequent endeavors led him to the ancient texts of Hellenistic Greece and imperial Rome, in which he detected very different ideas about what form a healthy or productive sexual and erotic life might take. Not all the ideas held by these historical societies are necessarily preferable to ones that we hold—not least in the manner in which women were socially positioned—but Foucault's research revealed the important variances about ideas about sexuality that humans hold, depending on the place and time they live.[1]

The historical dimension of queer theory, then, results from the field's rejection of an unchanging, static, "natural" sexuality or gendering which the historical record fails to affirm, and the discussion of *Brokeback Mountain* offered in this book is intended to historicize the ideas about sexuality and gender that the film bases its depictions upon as well as to foreground the critical and theoretical frameworks through which we can make sense of its depictions of life in the latter twentieth-century western United States as well as through our present moment.

History within the framework of queer theory, then, is not simply the question of what happened in the past, although it is concerned with obtaining as accurate a picture of prior eras as is possible; history, however, is also about how the historical stories that we tell ourselves about the past shape the ways we think about our own moment. For example, we frequently like to think that we find our freedom in our capacity for sexual and gender expression, and indeed we do, but where does the idea that sexuality is liberatory come from? What is it that we are seeking liberation from? Is the idea of such liberation a historically contingent one (i.e., one that pertains to certain societies at particular moments)?

Continuing on this line of inquiry, are we warranted to assume that the liberatory model of sexuality and gender is pertinent to all societies even in the present moment? It might come as an uncomfortable discovery to think that what we consider to be a central organizing historical, theoretical, and political project is not a one-size-fits-all endeavor, and that queer people in different spaces require their own explanations, histories, and projects as they define them.

There are two additional dimensions to how we can best understand the nature of historical thought within queer theory, and these relate to the history of the field itself. Two of the key lessons to be taken from the history of queer theory are, first, how it can be understood as a legacy and companion to feminist intellectual work and feminist activism and, second, how it relates to the global health pandemic that is HIV/AIDS.

Regarding the first legacy, queer theory bears a debt to a number of cognate fields whose modes of knowledge production have provided the needed tools for intellectual work, but probably no intellectual and political enterprise has shaped queer theory more than that of feminism. Feminist critiques of the circumstances of women's lives within dominant patriarchal societies have produced some of the most influential writing and activism in the past century and a half, and its debates and interventions continue into the present moment. Feminism's insistent linkage of intellectual work and political activism has formed one of the most important models for social transformation, and it has built much of the toolkit that queer theory has adapted for its own needs.

Before there was even a nascent idea about the political and social status of LGBQT people and their representation in the field of the social world or popular and literary cultures, the earliest feminist writers and activists were beginning to question the exclusion of women from the public arena of politics, finance, policy, cultural production, and education, to name a few of the spheres in which men of dominant race or class have enjoyed privileges unavailable to women. Among twentieth century's major historical political projects—which would include the struggle against totalitarianism, decolonization, and race politics, and the civil rights movements, class conflicts, and demands for economic justice—feminism has fought to make clear the stakes involved in the liberation of women.

Yet, the projects of feminism and queer theory are not identical because, while the questions that each project asks are similar, the individuals and groups on whose behalf they ask those questions are not entirely the same. This disparity comes into focus when we remember that the inclusion of men—queer and gay cis-gendered men and trans men—within the acronym "LGBQT" identifies a political project different from that of feminism. Yet, if the projects are different, they have historically overlapped through the debates within lesbian feminism about the need for all feminist projects to include lesbians—as well as women of color and working-class women. The passionate debates among feminists in the 1970s about lesbian feminism could well be understood as an inaugural moment for queer theory because the question of "What is a woman?" demanded new modes of thinking beyond what were understood as "essentialist" definitions based on reproduction, child-rearing, and domestic life.[2]

Crucial as a basis for queer theory, lesbian feminist critiques argued that some feminist ideas about how to define a woman could inadvertently reenforce dominant notions that tied being a woman to being straight, in a heterosexual marriage or having children (although, of course, lesbians could do both those latter things). These exclusions mirrored, for lesbians, the more general exclusion of lesbian sexuality from discussions of women's sexuality because, within the normative ideas of medicine, sexology, and psychoanalysis and psychology, women's sexuality remained unexplainable or it seems not to have existed in the first place. And, within the male-centric definitions of what defined sexual practice and sexual pleasure, that makes sense: women's bodies and women's being in the world are different from men's. But, the often risible assumptions made by science about the sexual experiences and behavior of women, be they straight, lesbian, bisexual, or asexual, made clear that the basis of what was considered "normal" (and therefore normative) was that of straight men's lives. As Annamarie Jagose writes, "Historically speaking . . . the masculine relation to sexuality has been figured differently from the feminine." This, as Jagose points out, is because "access to employment and an independent income has been both easier and more profitable for men than for women and, in criminal law, homosexuality has been constituted almost exclusively as a masculine proclivity."[3]

This last point helps us to understand how queer theory arose in the discovery that the meanings of same-sex sexuality for men and for women are quite different. As Jeffrey Weeks argues, "Lesbians and gays are not two genders within one sexual category. They have different histories, which are differentiated because of the complex organization of male and female identities, precisely along lines of gender."[4] That the medical and legal definitions of homosexuality frequently exempted women from being identified as such, and the fact that feminist thinkers and activists in the second-wave feminist movements of the 1960s and 1970s seemed to replicate this assumption inaugurated the critiques that became foundational to queer theory.

Concurrently, the gay rights political and social movements that emerged in the 1970s advocated strongly for the dignity of gay and lesbian people and the reformation of laws and institutional practices that discriminated against them; because of this, the gay movement would have seemed the appropriate place for lesbians to find political allies in their own intellectual and political projects, but, much to the chagrin of the movement, it probably reproduced some of the most egregiously sexist and exclusionary versions of male privilege that the mostly white men associated with the movement could take advantage of. This is not to say that there were no lesbians or people of color within the larger gay rights movement of the post-Stonewall period of the 1970s, but that the importance of their needs and demands was not always assumed to be as central to the political project as those of mostly white, often affluent men.

This disparity posed significant and vitalizing challenges to the gay rights movement that abide, and while the condensation of the categories of lesbian-gay-bisexual-queer-trans into the now institutionalized abbreviation "LGBQT" (which this book uses) might seem to dissolve the differences among those names, the fact is that queer theory sits at the tension point among them and derives its energies from those very tensions. Indeed, one of the central challenges to LGBQT intellectual and political projects has been to address these profound differences—among and between lesbian, gay, bisexual, queer, and trans people. Worth keeping in mind as one engages the field is that the questions that queer theorists pose are not necessarily the same, but they stem from the same call for justice and the same investigation of history and representation (including cinema) to discover where the discriminatory practices of anti-queer thought have been sustained.

Yet, if one historical moment can be seen to draw together many of the intellectual and political concerns of queer theory, that moment would be the swift emergence of HIV/AIDS into contemporary life. Beginning in the early 1980s, HIV forced a new mobilization of alliances among LGBQT people in ways that could not have been anticipated because HIV provided the opportunity for some of the most toxic of antiqueer, and specifically antigay-male, ideas and policies to take hold and to shape, quite directly, public policy, health, and governmental and institutional practices. No aspect of the lives of the men and women affected by the virus and its outcomes could remain untouched by the nourishment that homophobic thought received from the fear and rejection which HIV/AIDS evinced.

If the virus attacked the immune systems of those who were infected with it—who were not, it's worth reminding ourselves, not solely gay-identified men—the mediations of the virus attacked the very institutions that could serve those who were affected by HIV/AIDS and the repercussions were devastating, not least because the delays in identifying the virus and its effects might have been avoided had the crisis been perceived to be more urgent. We can never know.

What we can know, though, is that the HIV/AIDS crisis did not solely coincide with the development of queer theory but was rather one instance—and a powerful one—that allowed for the relations of power to sexuality and gender to become more discernible and to be seen in more explicit fashion as the governing and dominant homophobic assumptions about same-sex male sexuality took hold. As Jagose describes it,

"The most frequently cited context for queer in this sense is the network of activism and theory generated by the AIDS epidemic, parts of which have found that queer offers a rubric roomy and assertive enough for political intervention."

Jagose identifies some of the most important ways in which these interventions took shape in light of the new forms of public anti-queer thought, such as the pressure on how biomedical discourse thinks about the patient, the need for public discussions of sexual practices and the misrecognition of AIDS as a "gay disease," the need for coalitional politics to address the crisis, and the sense that the discourses about the disease shape the manner in which individuals and groups respond to it.

2. *Theoretical*: If a theory is understood as an explanation for phenomena, what are the theories of sexuality and gender that are available to us? For example, similar to the way in which the theory of evolution provides a powerful conceptual tool for scientists who study life to explain how change comes about in species, in populations, and in ecosystems, queer theory seeks within the humanities and the human social sciences to understand and to explain how gender and sexuality—especially those aspects of such kind that are deemed in conventional forms of thought as nonnormative or "perverse"—are regulated and subjugated for a larger project of domination.

For example, a typical "commonsense" explanation often circulated in the name of normative, heterosexual-privileging thinking is to claim that gender and sexuality are categories that come to humans from the natural world. Given that our genitals are used in the reproduction of new humans, this logic runs, we should assume that our sexualities and our genders should always be organized around the ostensible goal of reproduction.

This theory—for that is what it is—assumes that the purpose of our bodies is to reproduce (as opposed, say, to having pleasure) and that all other sexual activities and thinking are secondary to this ostensibly "natural" sexuality.

By proxy, it also assumes that all other sexualities other than those dedicated to reproduction are unacceptable if indeed not repugnant. Also by proxy, it assumes that only those forms of sexuality that are sanctioned to sustain such reproductive sexuality are worthwhile, and those forms of normative gendering are intended to facilitate reproduction. Any manner of gendering that seems contrary to such is thus construed as unhealthy or even monstrous.

If this theory might sound far-fetched, it should be recalled that, within the United States, it has formed the basis of many political and institutional decisions over the past half century, from the US government's policy beginning in the 1950s (and continuing for three decades) to terminate any governmental employee whose sexuality was, mysteriously, deemed "perverse," to the exclusion of LGBQT personnel from serving in the armed forces under the bizarre regulations called "don't ask, don't tell," to the current legislative assault on and harassment of trans people in their use of public toilets.

Queer theory, then, theorizes why a society has such controversies within itself and asks what the implications are for the outcomes of such debates. As we will see, the meanings that we attach to what might seem issues restricted to sexuality and gender are often clues to larger assumptions and ideas being made about all manner of ways in which power, subjectivity, and social life operate, thus putting queer theory at the heart of debates that are larger than its specific questions and modes of inquiry in scope.

3. *Textual*: A significant challenge of engaging with the historical and theoretical dimensions of human social life within the domains of sexuality and gender is to discover the techniques by which societies mediate their ideas about sexuality and gender within their representational practices. That is, how does any society, our own included, write, speak, and represent its ideas about sex or gender? These textual questions are ones about the silences and techniques of evasion from discovery at work in so many queer people's lives, while,

simultaneously they are also about discovering that, in the past century and a half, the topics of sexuality and gender have developed into an immense field of inquiry that has not always been benign toward LGBQT people.

Thus, the textual modes of queer life often require dissident sexual subjects to move carefully through life and to be careful in the way that they discuss their sexuality and their gendering. When, for example, the Hollywood corporations that produce film for mass audiences began in the early 1930s to abide by the Production Code, they installed a careful and nuanced set of rules that were to make clear, explicitly and tacitly, that any form of sexuality not seen as "wholesome," heterosexually compulsive and organized through ideals of white, protestant, and middle-class life and marriage were prohibited from inclusion in the Hollywood cinema.

The American corporate film industry would abide by these rules for the next four decades, and the impact upon the text of the films made then was immense. Almost no mention is made of the existence of lesbians or gay men in the many films manufactured by the industry and those few exceptions in which a depiction of such figures does occur finds them rendered as weak, pathetic, mentally unstable, cruel, unreliable, and pernicious. In many ways, such representations were worse than being excluded entirely from the film texts made by Hollywood.

Even more remarkable, though, is that our historical knowledge of the film industry in this period tells us that there were many queer people—and nonqueer people sympathetic to their situation—involved in the making of such films. We might be tempted to see these queer people as somehow complicit in their own subjection (we probably should be more sympathetic to their situation and admiring of their bravery), but in fact they were probably leaving textual clues to the presence of their labor in implicit ways that it requires us to be sensitive in our interpretations to what the texts are saying.

In the field of queer theory, one way of becoming sensitive to these clues has been in relation to the topic of "camp," which is the name given historically to the manner in which gay men and lesbians used wit, irony, and textual play to allow a text to say multiple things at once, not least about the presence of queer desire and sexuality being in the world. These kinds of textual clues contained within camp play might not be immediately obvious to the casual viewer—they were intended to be capable of evasion and to be denied for homophobic viewers—and often they operate through stylistic markers and subtle plays of metaphor and allegory.[5] Their ability to do two seemingly contrary things at once—to affirm the presence of queer people in the world as at least not malignant and to deny that this very affirmation is taking place—makes the work of the queer theorist challenging to the degree that she or he must maintain a sensitive eye and ear to moments of ambiguity and multivalence within a text.

A parallel and co-constituting way of thinking about the textual work of queer theory develops in terms of how anti-queer forms of thought and practice have fostered their own kinds of textual analysis in order to detect—and often, invent—what such homophobic kinds of imagination think queers are saying, writing, and thinking. Such investigations are often couched in euphemism and indirection themselves, seeking as they do to avoid the most overt accusations of malfeasance and violent intent. These kinds of textual modes speak on behalf of purportedly threatened populations of heterosexual men, women, and children who are said to be menaced by the very presence of queer people in the world. Thus, the queer theorist must be sensitive in a different way to the subtleties of the text, where he or she seeks to identify the operations of power and domination as they work to regulate, exclude, and sometimes simply name queer people.

Complicating matters even more in this matter of the textuality of queer theory is the fact that the two manners of thinking about queer signification—the queer-positive and the homophobic—engage each other, often most intensely in the most volatile periods of attempts for social control of queer sexualities and genders. We can get a sense of how this works when we consider the fact that the idea of the existence of

a person called a "homosexual" has not appeared until quite
recently in human history (as is discussed below in chapter
one.) While there undoubtedly have long existed same-sex
sexual acts in human societies, the invention of this category
of social being occurred not in the context of any individual
queer person or a queer community needing this name; it
emerged as medical science sought to invent a taxonomy of
human sexual behaviors and decided that a set of acts should
be attached to a name—"the homosexual"—in ways that
ultimately probably disallowed for a more nuanced and varied
idea of how sexuality and gender work for individual women
and men and for the relations among them.

This nomination's blindness to subtlety, though, provided
for the emergent modern subcultures in the west to begin
to coalesce in large cities such as London, Berlin, and New
York and to reinvent the city as not only a place where such
dissident sexual cultures could develop and provide for like-
minded people—including straight people who felt themselves
to be eccentric—but also a place of community and inclusion.

Now, a comment on the modes of textual analysis contained
within the broad configuration that is queer theory. There are
many ways in which the scholars and writers associated with
queer theory examine the materials that allow them to study
the meanings of sexuality and gender, including ethnography
and interview techniques, archival discovery and historical
research, discourse analysis and ideological critique, semiotics,
literary analysis, media analysis, legal scholarship, bioethics,
and journalism. Each technique has its own set of protocols
and practices, and in many fields there are expectations
about how best to engage with the relevant phenomena and
materials. If, as mentioned earlier, the field has always had
to be highly interdisciplinary, it has also had often to prove
its merits within its respective institutional settings such as
departments and research institutes.

The sheer breadth of such research practices indicates the
vitality of the field, but it also means that simply for need of
brevity the present account in this book is constrained to do

justice to all the activities and intellectual productions that emerge from queer theory. As the following chapters hope to make clear, there are key foundational figures whose work has shaped so much of the work in queer theory and an absence of knowledge about them would make any discussion of the subject direly incomplete. Simultaneously, there are a large number of thinkers and writers about whom another volume—really, a set of volumes—would augment the present account in important and vital ways. Where appropriate, their work is included here, but research in anthropology, sociology, literary studies, legal studies, etc., could not be included simply because of constraint of space.

Further, the intent of the book is to help readers who are unfamiliar with queer theory to gain insight into the ways in which it sheds light on the workings of a popular cinematic text: *Brokeback Mountain*. Any number of other films might serve to make sense of queer theory, and each of them would yield different understandings of the enterprises of queer theory. Indeed, the reader will hopefully embark on her or his own analysis of other such films as a way of extending the work presented here and to begin to perform the work of queer theory within their own intellectual life.

The choice of *Brokeback Mountain* for this book presents important opportunities and significant constraints for limning the contours of the field of queer theory because, as regards the former, the sheer popularity of the film and the centrality of Lee's film to debates in queer theory and media studies lend it an accessibility that is meant be of aid to the reader. Further, there are other films whose critique in the terms of queer theory would be sources of rich understanding, but the challenges to access some of them could daunt the reader who comes to the field with fresh eyes.

One of the most important constraints that the choice of this particular film places on this book's account of queer theory is that of the white and male-centric nature of this particular queer narrative, and my hope is that the reader can orient himself or herself within the theoretical and critical terms on hand to see the interpretive value of this film. That said, there remains the simple truth that the women characters in *Brokeback Mountain* play a secondary role to the same-sex male and masculinist story in which Ennis del Mar and Jack Twist have the defining and most complicated and nuanced roles. A long roster of other films would illuminate the more complicated range of questions about queer theory's critiques of gender and sexuality and would include more prominently women, trans and bisexual characters, and queer women and men of color.

The role that feminism has played within the inception and the development of queer theory becomes prominent in the account that follows, and this, I hope, offsets the sense that Lee's film might weigh more heavily toward solely seeing men and male eroticism as the centerpiece of LGBQT concerns. The latter is hardly the case, and indeed feminism's concerns with how women's lives are shaped by injustice and exclusion are extended within queer theory's ethical commitment to understanding how anti-queer violence mirrors and duplicates many of the techniques of misogyny.

One of the most vital intersections of queer theory is that with critiques of race and racism and, again, the choice of film here for discerning the convergence between analyses of sexuality/gender and race present challenges in a film that calls so little attention to its racial depictions—especially as those depictions are eclipsed by its (apparently) scandalous sexuality. But, we are never one thing or the other: we are not either sexed or assigned racial categories, we do not have either a gender or a race. Rather, we inhabit these names simultaneously, and an important concern for this book has been to remind the reader to attend to sexuality and gender as they are racial categories.

With that understood, it is also important to emphasize the fact that this book examines a film, as opposed to a literary text, a legal case, a historical document, or a piece of journalism, and this means that the discussions of cinema in this book will inevitably eclipse the way that a scholar examining the work of a lesbian poet, or a legal case regarding transgender rights might consider those matters. There are, however, important advantages to organizing this book's discussion around an instance of cinema.

Cinema has been a key modern technology of representation that has shaped many of our most powerful ideas about sexuality and gender for a wide variety of audiences. Some of the ideas have been highly pernicious to queer people, as discussed above in terms of the Hollywood Production Code, but film has also offered a chance for queer sexualities and genders to find the space of fantasy and self-invention.

Film does not require of its viewers the meeting of often immense challenges of access that a literary text or historical monograph does, in terms of educational opportunities and in terms of communities of affiliation to read and interpret those modes of textual production. Film has historically been widely accessible and therefore has been a medium in which many queer people have gained the first inklings of the possibilities that new kinds of sexuality and gender might become a reality within their lives.

However, we should not assume that a film—any film—is transparent in its operations and in the ways it seeks to represent the world to its audiences. This is how the aforementioned question of textuality in queer theory comes into play here. Such an assumption is dangerous because film, like any cultural medium, contains within it ideas and techniques that demand our critical and analytical attention. Indeed, the more seemingly obvious a sense of the world a film seems to offer us, especially when it employs the technique of realism, the more urgent it is that we take the time to discover the various elements that constitute its uniquely mediated labors. Those elements include its mise-en-scène, editing, sound and music, dialogue, actor performance, etc.

Many of these techniques of realist cinema[6] are organized to assure the viewer of a certain way of viewing the world in the most explicit sense of how film is a visual medium, but "viewing" also can be understood in the ideological sense: that no matter how innocent (or banal) a message might seem to be inscribed within the sights and sounds of film, they are powerful indicators of how a culture is thinking about any number of issues at hand. Realist cinema—that is, the cinema which seeks to foster the sense within the viewer that she or he is looking at the "real world" rather than a photographic representatiòn of it—organizes the spectator's experience in such a way that she or he is not disoriented when interpreting the three dimensions of space on a two-dimensional screen. One of the most effective ways of achieving that orientation is to anchor the viewer's experience in relation to a primary character through whose eyes we, the viewers, discover the world within the film.

Critics have argued about how such "identification," as this is called, is needed for realist cinema to achieve its desired results, but one of the most powerful critiques that has shaped critical discussions of film in the past four decades argues that this identificatory dynamic is highly gendered. In *Visual Pleasure and Narrative Cinema*, Laura Mulvey argues that there are three modes of looking that are contained in the cinema: first, that of the camera at the action that is recorded; second, that of the characters within the film at each other; and third, that of the spectator at the screen.

The manner in which the Hollywood realist film prioritizes these looks tells us much about how this kind of film wants us to view, and according to Mulvey, the realist cinema uses the camera's look to subtly prioritize the look of a particular kind of character who gazes at another person within the film's mise-en-scène. That character who looks, not coincidentally, is male and the object of his look is a woman whom he gazes upon with desire. That same woman herself does not gaze with a corresponding desire and in fact is not represented as capable of such a desiring gaze, the result of which is that there is a tremendous asymmetry in the organization of looking within the realist film, an asymmetry born of sexual and gender difference. In short, within the realist cinema, men look and women are looked at.

Mulvey's theory of the gaze was based upon her analysis of the films produced in the Classical period of the Hollywood studio system (spanning the years 1917–1960), and it is the case that the gendered aspects of looking have altered over time, with the emergence of different ways or "regimes" of looking within the moving image. While there are numerous instances in which, contra the structured looking which Mulvey theorized, women, queer men, or trans men and women are said to possess the gaze—that is their desire is affirmed through the techniques of cinema—the bulk of the popular culture remains in the thrall to the powerful look accorded to heteronormative longing within the dominant cinema. For that reason, this book hopefully will provide an account of how queer theory's critiques are of aid to understanding the sway that films can have over their spectators and to provide necessary tools for critically examining the representation of queer sexuality and gender within film.

One of the blossomings of queer theory, in fact, has been within the area of film, television, and media studies, and I encourage the reader to discover the writing of queer media theorists whose work has had an immense impact upon the study of the moving image. A list of further reading appears at the back of this book. Among these critics, the work of Gary Needham's book of the same name on the topic of *Brokeback Mountain* provides a more expansive account of the production history of the film as an independent film in the global cinema. Needham's book has shaped much of the present account, and the primary hope for the book you are holding in your hands—to introduce the reader to queer theory through the film—is to offer the reader the tools of queer critique to analyze the film.

As I have written this book, a number of friends and colleagues—gay and lesbian, of a certain generation over the age of fifty—have told me how difficult the term "queer" is for them to hear in any version that is not intended to insult and harm LGBQT men and women. These comments remind me that the historical era in which the hate-filled epithet "queer"—along with a longer list of other insults—abides with us. When I have responded to these reminders by asking my friends and colleagues whether the term might be repurposed in order to defend against such harm, their pain and disgust is so deep and real that the answer is a "no." As this book arrives in the reader's hands, it does so with the wish that it might prevent future LGBQT brothers and sisters from living through anti-queer forms of pain.

Notes

1 Michel Foucault, *The Use of Pleasure: The History of Sexuality*, *Volume 2*, trans. Robert Hurley (New York: Vintage Books, 1988) and Michel Foucault, *The Care of the Self: The History of Sexuality*, *Volume 3*, trans. Robert Hurley (New York: Vintage Books, 1988).

2 For a fuller and illuminating account of the lesbian feminist debates as they relate to queer theory, see Annamarie Jagose, *Queer Theory: An Introduction* (New York: New York University Press, 1996).

3 Ibid., 45.

4 Jeffrey Weeks, *Sexuality and Its Discontents: Meanings, Myths and Modern Sexualities* (London: Routledge and Kegan Paul, 1985), 203.

5 Matthew Tinkcom, *Working Like a Homosexual: Camp, Capital, Cinema* (Durham: Duke University Press, 2003).

6 Other kinds of cinema, such as avant-garde, experimental, and art cinemas, engage with queer sexualities and genders as well, but here the critical emphasis will be upon dominant narrative cinema.

CHAPTER ONE

Queer theory

*People will ask themselves why we were so bent on
ending the rule of silence regarding what was the
noisiest of our preoccupations.*

MICHEL FOUCAULT[1]

Queer epistemology

In order to understand how queer theory has transformed the
manner in which we think about gender and sexuality, we can
begin with the writings of French philosopher, historian, and
activist Michel Foucault. Writing in the 1960s, 1970s, and
1980s, Foucault argued that sexuality has become the central
defining force in modern social life, and its regulation—by
governments, by institutions (including marriage), and by
individuals—has achieved what no other kind of practice in
human history had been able to do: to convince every individual
that his or her liberation and self-expression of who he or she
is relies upon the constant and repeated telling of one's sexual
life, be it imagined (i.e., the source of fantasy which might
never be acted upon) or enacted (i.e., the manner in which one
uses one's body to say "who it is that one really is.")

Foucault's research examined the development of contemporary institutions such as schools, universities, hospitals,

clinics, prisons, and law courts, among others, in order to discover how each of these places played a role in the ongoing development and refinement of the techniques used to nurture the perception that humans could and should somehow be liberated from the constraints that they might feel put upon them by saying what it is that they *sexually* desired and how an identity—"the homosexual," "the pervert," "the lesbian"—would be the name through which to make claims to free such people from social rebuke, calumny, persecution, attack, arrest, and murder.

It should be clear that the claim here is not that Foucault is the first modern philosopher or theorist to examine the role that sexuality plays in our lives, and indeed Foucault's work should be situated in response to the proliferation of discussion and writing about sexuality that appeared in the one hundred years leading up to his work. In the middle of the nineteenth century in Europe, doctors, researchers, and others in the domain of medicine began to study sexuality in the terms of scientific practice: to provide taxonomies and explanations for the different sexual acts in which humans engage and discussions of how those acts—and the desires for or repulsions from them—figure in the stories we tell about ourselves. Central figures in this scientific practice—Richard von Krafft-Ebing, Magnus Hirschfeld, Havelock Ellis et al.—conceived of sexuality as a prime instance of how post-Enlightenment science could produce knowledge in ways that had not hitherto been possible. In their work, they sought out men and women—and, key to this, particularly women—whose sexual lives did not conform to conventional notions of what they perceived to be healthy sexual activity, especially as such norms were conjoined with the capacity to reproduce. The sense of these early "sexologists," as they were called, was that human sexuality included a wide range of activities which the biological capacity to reproduce did not explain and their research was devoted to illuminating the multiple kinds of sex and sexualities which humans engaged in—even as many of these forms of sexuality had strong prohibitions and punishments often attached to the public knowledge of them.

The early sexologists—and we should include here most prominently the Austrian doctor and writer Sigmund Freud (1856–1939)—thought themselves to have discovered a vast and exciting new domain of human life which, to their minds, had not been examined with any rigor and which, properly understood, might help men and women to illuminate how and why sex was so important to humans beyond the biological need to reproduce humans. The project of early sexology was to classify and describe all variety of sexual activities among humans with, to their minds, as little judgment or prescription as possible about what kinds of human sexuality were "normal" or "abnormal." However, despite this impulse toward seeming scientific non-bias, it was probably inevitable that their own assumptions about sexuality would emerge in the course of their research, and nowhere is this as clear as it is with the work of Freud and the activity of his theories of what he called "psychoanalysis."

Freud's first publication in this new area was *The Interpretation of Dreams* in 1900, and it would be difficult to overemphasize the impact that this book has had on how we think about ourselves. In that book—and in the many additional works that Freud published up until his death— he claimed that the human mind was organized around the development in human infants of a capacity to repress all that was harsh and diminishing of life, and this repression was made possible by the unconscious aspects of our minds. The unconscious, for Freud, filled itself with the impressions of everything we resisted, recognizing the damage it caused to our sense of ourselves and it developed early in the life of infants in the social life of the family. For Freud, the most notable trauma that inaugurates the unconscious within each individual is the loss of a primary and defining bond, that between infant and mother. The bond with the mother nurtures the infant without prohibitions as to when the baby might sleep, eat, or defecate, and when it comes to pass that the infant must begin to adhere to social norms of life—including the adoption of language in order to communicate—the child experiences a profound and life-defining partition from the human who has most devoted herself to the child's well-being.

This partition, according to Freud, sets into motion the development of the unconscious as it makes possible our ability to live with loss and difficulty, but the unconscious keeps a hidden record, so to speak, held within our minds and emerging within key moments of everyday life such as the telling of jokes or unexpected slips of tongue, but it is most notably when we dream that the unconscious discloses something apparently hidden about ourselves. For Freud, our dreams reveal to us those experiences—even as recent as from the past day—which we might not willfully have recognized as they directly caused the suffering they instill in us, and it is in dreaming that they return (often in highly disguised form) for us to reconcile ourselves to them and to continue living, despite our pain. Most of us, Freud thought, live with our neuroses with the aid of the unconscious mind, but for some men and women the pain that resides within the unconscious is so unbearable that it comes to dominate the mental life of the individual for reasons he or she cannot understand. Indeed, this pain is so profound that the unconscious resists its discovery lest it brings back to us the difficult thoughts and experiences that we are so assiduously resisting. Thus, such men and women experience physical and mental pain for which there seems no cause by disease or infection and it is the activity of psychoanalysis—explicitly, the analysis of the mind with the aid of the doctor—which can reveal under safe and unjudging circumstances what these traumas are and how they are indeed not capable of hurting or destroying us.

Freud thought that the discovery of the unconscious, as it is shaped by trauma, was key to the emancipation of humans from those thoughts—be they memories, fantasies, fears, or desires—that harm them, but along the way he came to consider how what the unconscious holds within it are not solely traumatic experiences from real life but, additionally, fantasies, desires, and revulsions that the individual does not want to consider himself or herself capable of. These fantasies, as Freud's patients disclosed them to him, were often specifically sexual or related to sexuality, and from this Freud concluded that such thoughts revealed aspects of ourselves that defined us without our necessarily knowing it. For Freud and those working in the psychoanalytic practice, the analysand (the patient undergoing treatment) frequently lived within a deep contradiction of *both* desiring sexual acts that the larger society might deem unacceptable while concurrently not actually knowing that they held such fantasies or desires within their mental lives. Psychoanalysis could help the patient to perceive how such traumas and fantasies could be revealed without necessarily damaging the patient and simultaneously realize that such thoughts probably had some root cause which was not necessarily about the fantasy per se, but were in fact the expression of some other idea or experience. Thus, the contradiction could be explained and the patient could, by way of the "talking cure" as Freud called it, begin to recover with new insight about that which had afflicted them.

The psychoanalytic patient, then, needed to speak at length with his or her psychoanalyst in order to consider all those possible sources for troubling—that is, "neurotic"—unconscious ideas that were making the patient ill without seeming cause. In a series of remarkable case studies (which are well worth reading, as they are as compelling as any good novel) Freud narrated the process through which he thought he had aided his patients in uncovering the sources of their anguish, often about their sexual desires and fantasies and often which were related most directly to the traumas of personal and family life. Importantly for this account, Freud sensed that the larger culture prohibited men and women from recognizing how deeply sexualized life is, even when it is not about the most obvious forms of genital activity but is more about form of intimacy and association with others which the culture denigrates or denies. Freud thought that it was only by talking at length—in the privacy of the doctor's or therapist's office—that we would begin to understand how such repressed thought shapes our behavior and experiences of the world.

The sexological assumption about the increased need for discussions about sexuality thus provides the foundation for Foucault's later intervention into the discussion because Foucault called this unexpected turn of events in modern societies—that is, the expansion of psychoanalytic explanations and concepts to many people who may not undergo psychoanalytic treatment but nevertheless employ the concepts of psychoanalysis in everyday life—"the repressive hypothesis." By this, Foucault meant that the dominant way of thinking about gender and sexuality in the West—that we have been prohibited from speaking and writing about sexuality—developed in the previous century under the auspices of the assumptions of psychoanalysis. At the heart of these practices, Foucault claimed, was the insistence that those women and men who felt themselves to suffer mentally should begin talking about their interior lives in order to find relief and, most central to psychoanalysis and psychology, the assumption that what was repressed by the mind—most vitally its sexual ideas and impulses—should be discovered and articulated. In this frame of thinking was the assumption that societies insisted upon the exclusion of sexual thinking, speaking and acting from, at the very least, public conversation, and this was alleged to have created a sense that sexuality was a secret that every individual bore and, when unhealthily neglected or repressed, it led to suffering and illness. Thus, the role of psychoanalysis and its institutional heirs was to provide the venue in which such a suffering individual might, in violation of such prohibitions on speaking about sexuality, say what it was that he or she needed to express about their sexual desires and practices. The talking cure was the most significant achievement that would allow for sexuality to be set loose from its inhibitions and instead be made a source of freedom and well-being.

Foucault's theories turned sexology's ideas upside down by arguing that there had hardly ever been the limits on sexual discussion that Freud and those working in his legacy claimed were the case; indeed, according to Foucault, the role that the talking cure played in the development of contemporary ideas about sexuality functioned toward the seemingly ever-expanding presence that larger institutions, most notably the state, played in the control of how humans think about themselves and their relations to one another. Key to Foucault's ideas about sexuality was the sense that, while sexuality so strongly seems to be at its foundation a biological function and thus might seem to be consistent across all human societies, in point of fact sexuality is contingent upon the cultural meanings attached to such biology and is thus not timeless but rather dependent on a variety of ideas about the cultural meanings of sexuality and gender. Indeed for Foucault, sexuality is *produced* by humans rather than it being simply inherent in them, and Foucault asserted that the repressive hypothesis has emerged in contemporary societies as an elegant tool with which to develop ever more refined categories and techniques for the regulation of individuals through the incitation to talk about their sexuality.

As Nikki Sullivan comments, for Foucault, "Sexuality is not natural but, rather, is discursively constructed . . . experienced, and understood in culturally and historically specific ways."[2] That is, as long as citizens were talking—and talking and talking—about their sexual fantasies, needs, repulsions, and curiosities—they would be participating in practices and their related languages—what Foucault called "discourses"—that allowed them to consider themselves liberated all the while that they were accepting the terms through which this liberation was made possible (and, to be frank, had limits set upon it). As Foucault wrote,

> Through the various discourses, legal sanctions against minor perversions were multiplied; sexual irregularity was annexed to mental illness; from childhood to old age,

a norm of sexual development was defined and all the possible deviations were carefully described; pedagogical controls and medical treatments were organized; around the least fantasies, moralists, but especially doctors, brandished the whole emphatic vocabulary of abomination. All this garrulous attention which has us in a stew over sexuality, is it not motivated by one basic concern: to ensure population, to reproduce labor capacity, to perpetuate the form of social relations: in short, to constitute a sexuality that is economically useful and politically conservative.[3]

Within Foucault's analysis, the manner in which sexuality had come to be framed in industrialized Western settings ultimately and tacitly linked ideas about "normal" and "abnormal" sexualities to whether they were productive and reproductive. Further, it conjoined sexuality with economic questions of how nations might expand their populations in the competition among such nations for wealth and prosperity. Whatever kinds of sex that did not contribute to the expansion of the populace and the mobilization of labor markets for economic growth was deemed unacceptable (Foucault's "politically conservative"); however, this was not enacted in the moral terms of religion (the role of churches' regulating sexual morality having been on the decline since the advent of scientific Enlightenment) but through the techniques of sexology and psychoanalysis as they were empowered by states and governments to define the "emphatic vocabulary of abomination." This expansion of the state was a part of what Foucault called "biopower": the ability of states and those working on their behalf to say what forms of sexuality should be encouraged (most notably for the expansion of the economy: families should have enough children to produce new participants for labor markets, for example) and which should be discouraged.

Foucault argued that the ability of the various institutions that develop and administer these new forms of sexual regulation derives its power from their capacity to take advantage of a prior-going practice: that of confession within religion. Although religion (and here Foucault has in mind Roman Catholicism) had ceded to science much of its power to explain and regulate many dimensions of life, including that of sexuality, its nuanced practices of confession offered a way of producing discourse, in writing and in speech, about sexuality which medicine and science found useful. This adaptation of confession—from the confessional within the church to that at the doctor's office and the therapist's couch—realigned the act of confession from one in which the penitent sought absolution and forgiveness to one in which the patient was now endlessly detailing how he or she felt, thought, fantasized, and enacted his or her sexual thoughts and impulses, but paradoxically without any ultimate release or absolution. Confession had become, according to Foucault, an unceasing activity because "the obligation to confess is now relayed through so many different points, is so deeply ingrained in us, that we no longer perceive it as the effect of a power that constrains us." Quite the contrary, Foucault insisted, "it seems to us that truth, lodged in our most secret nature, 'demands' only to surface; that if it fails to do so, this is because a constraint holds it in place, the violence of a power weighs it down, and it can finally be articulated only at the price of a kind of liberation."[4]

Thus, we are encouraged to develop and refine our capacity to speak about sexuality in ever more elaborate terms; Foucault comments that "it is no longer a question simply of saying what was done—the sexual act—and how it was done; but of reconstructing, in and around the act, the thoughts that recapitulated it, the obsessions that accompanied it, the images, desires, modulations, and quality of the pleasure that animated it." This was a socially shared enterprise: "For the first time no doubt, a society has taken upon itself to solicit and hear the imparting of individual pleasures."[5]

Key within this statement is the phrase "imparting of individual pleasures," because the obligation to speak about one's sexuality was, for Foucault, a very subtle form of coercion whereby the person describing her or his desires, thoughts, and actions would think that such ideas were solely his or her own and not consider how the larger society was, to use Foucault's term, "imparting" to him or her the very language in which such ideas were to be articulated. In this regard, Foucault's theory of sexuality recognizes how deeply we are enmeshed in social relations that often seem to us benign and innocent but which, when considered in the larger set of possibilities of how we might live our lives, may restrict the sense of what is possible in the ways we live our lives, not least in terms of sexuality.

This way of thinking critically about the place of sexuality in contemporary life, though, includes both the regulatory and the liberatory, and it is the combination of these features that led Foucault to elaborate more generally about how he understood human social relations to operate because his work was centrally focused on political questions, that is, on questions of power. Foucault's rather brief discussion of power—it totals a few pages—suggests an innovative notion of power relations in society with characteristics different from how we might conventionally think about the matter. He argues that power is not a thing to be owned or exchanged, but a practice that binds individuals together; that those with socially inferior positions participate in power relations, even if it is to their disadvantage; and that power and its resistance co-constitute, rather than entirely antagonize, each other.[6]

Set against a tradition of thinking about power as a "top-down" hierarchy in which those with greater power impose it upon those with less power, without the latter's necessary consent or consultation (the model of power-as-domination), Foucault defines power in a more dispersed sense, where it is true that some individuals and institutions have more power than others but where it is important to remind ourselves that no one is ever entirely and finally deprived of one's ability to engage in power relations: to speak (or not). This, for Foucault, was because the modern state had ceded the right to deprive us of our life through execution, and thus we could still speak even under the worst of circumstances where the consequences for such speech would be dire.

For Foucault, the way that we participate in power is enacted less by direct coercion, where we have no choice in what we are directed to do, but rather through the sense that we can choose—but often only within limits which we see, paradoxically for Foucault, as opportunity. As he suggests, "The irony of this deployment is in having us believe that our 'liberation' is in the balance."[7] In terms of the theory of sexuality which he offers, individuals gain power by knowing the terms through which their sexuality is validated or denigrated and by learning to speak, with ever-increasing refinement, within the confessional mode in terms that gain for him or her the right to speak more. Further, Foucault's idea of power relations functions as a network of affiliations rather than as a hierarchy; in the latter model (which considers power more like the traditional military) a chain of command insists on adherence and obedience to what is ordained, and resistance is considered to be absolutely proscribed: either one performs the task one is ordered to do or one does not, and the latter can lead to dire consequences. In the Foucauldian model, individuals are making decisions about which forms of power they want to participate in, and most of us in contemporary societies understand the consequences of following the rule or not but can live with the outcomes nonetheless. (There are a few key exceptions about which Foucault himself was aware: prisoners, refugees, and those without documented national identity.)

We might ask why Foucault's theory of sexuality and power is necessary for queer theory, and the most direct answer is that it helps to make sense of how sexuality, which Foucault deems to be a central form of social participation, can simultaneously be both highly regulated (think of the emergence of sexology and psychiatry) and be the manner in which men and women express their nonadherence to what the larger society has deemed "normal" and "abnormal." If power is theorized solely in terms of coercion—the domination model—then would not most men and women live their sexuality in the most normative ways if nonnormative sexualities might bring severe penalties? Why would anyone live their sexuality in ways that give rise to condemnation or discipline? Foucault's answer is that sexuality is where individuals learn how to become empowered within the model that he offers, and that power is almost never absolute but that simultaneously it comes at a cost: that the very terms of identity—woman, gay, queer, trans, straight, bisexual—arise out of the very institutions that regulate them. Judith Butler comments about his theory that it "points out that juridical systems of power produce the subjects they subsequently come to represent." There are no men and women who are exterior to the regulatory systems of gender and sexuality prior to their encounters with the institutions that define normative terms; rather, according to Butler, "The subjects regulated by such structures are, by virtue of being subjected to them, formed, defined, and reproduced in accordance with the requirements of those structures."[8]

As Butler indicates, even our sense of freedom in our sexuality is something that, in part at least, is granted to us (which is what she means by its being "protected") rather than something we might have discovered and developed within ourselves. This reverses a more conventional notion of gender and sexuality as something innate within us that seeks to be expressed and, instead, it conceptualizes that what we might think is inborn and essential is in fact shaped by the social forces (what Foucault means by power) to offer us a place in the social field in which we might act, speak, and engage others.

As Annamarie Jagose describes Foucault's theory of power and sexuality, "Since he does not think that power is a fundamentally repressive force, Foucault does not endorse such liberationist strategies as breaking prohibitions and speaking out." We should be careful to see how Foucault himself has been accused of being conservative because, "as Foucault takes a resolutely anti-liberatory position on this matter he is sometimes read—perhaps unsurprisingly given the common currency of what he critiques as 'the repressive hypothesis'—as advocating political defeatism."[9]

Jagose points out that it would be a mistake to see Foucault's explanation for the relation between sexuality and power as solely "defeatist," and reminds us of the other, corresponding part of his theory—that sexuality is simultaneously creative inasmuch as it discovers those very limits which power establishes on what might be said—or not said—in the network of social relations. There is the possibility of resistance for Foucault, but it needs always to be aware of the sense that its most important possibilities can be anticipated by power relations in advance within the discourses available. As Jagose comments, "Foucault specifically instances how the category of homosexuality was formed in relation to structures of power and resistance. The rise of the homosexual as a 'species' exemplifies the polyvalent capacities of discourse."[10]

Key to this theory of sexuality that Foucault, before his death in 1984, began to develop in his landmark series of books, *The History of Sexuality,* was the idea that the role that sexuality plays in the lives of modern societies is *both* highly regulatory and highly liberatory, but that we must always keep in mind that it is not solely one or the other. Nor has this always been the case for all human societies; some cultures have not assigned this role to sexuality in the manner in which we do. In this way of thinking about gender and sexuality, we should be wary of the too-easy forms of identity (and its resistances) as they participate in the dynamics of state-sponsored biopower while simultaneously recognizing that men and women can invent new ways of relating to one another in the ways in which they live as gendered and sexual beings.

This combined status of sexual knowledge—as at once both the place of power over individuals and the place in which such individuals might create new kinds of social roles for themselves—is a different way of thinking about how we live within and know about the societies in which we live. Indeed, *how* we make knowledge (rather than *what* we claim to know) about ourselves and others, what philosophers have traditionally called epistemology, fosters a unique role for gender and sexuality in the self-definitions of individuals.

Eve Sedgwick and the epistemology of the closet

Building upon this theory, the American literary critic and theorist Eve Kosofsky Sedgwick developed what she called "the epistemology of the closet" in her book of that same name. In that book and in her other writings, Sedgwick offered the idea that one of the defining ways that women and men in the West think about themselves is not only in terms of the relation of power to sexuality that Foucault had in mind, but that the idea of the *closet* also shaped how we talk about that relation, no matter who we are. The closet—which can be understood as a metaphor for a place in which our sexuality hides from broader view and emerges within language, bodily acts, and social discourses—organizes the things we say and do in relation to our fantasies, aversions, and desires in our erotic lives, and it does so whether we identify as heterosexual or as gay, lesbian, bisexual, transgender, or queer.

Sedgwick asserts that "an understanding of virtually any aspect of modern Western culture must be, not merely incomplete, but damaged in its central substance to the degree that it does not incorporate critical analysis of modern homo/heterosexual definition,"[11] not least because the category of the "heterosexual" is meaningless with that of the "homosexual." According to Sedgwick, this "homo/heterosexual definition" organizes how each of us thinks and lives our gender and our sexuality no matter whether we are homosexual or heterosexual (to employ this particular distinction). Indeed, the fact that we think of ourselves as needing these categories for self-identification puts us into the very situation that Foucault has described, where particular names stand in for particular kinds of sexualities, and the people who associate with them are said to be liberated, all the while that those names are imposed from elsewhere and are historically recent phenomena, having only emerged in the European or American setting at the end of the nineteenth century. Indeed, it is a deep irony that the idea

QUEER THEORY   **39**

of the "homosexual"—a person whose sexual aim and interest
is sexual contact with someone of the same gender—appeared
before the idea of the "heterosexual" in Western discourses of
sexuality. This fact tells us much about how the names given to
sexualities and the people associated with them have developed
more quickly toward thinking about nonnormative kinds of
sexualities than about what ostensibly is thought to be typical.

Complicating matters is that, as Sedgwick notes, the
metaphor of the closet has become the way in which most men
and women learn to discuss their sexuality: as a secret that must
be disclosed under the right conditions to the right person. But,
it is also a way by which many individuals and institutions
maintain power over those men and women who are made to
feel that their sexuality is not "normal" or acceptable within
the dominant ways of thinking and feeling about gender and
sexuality. Thus, according to Sedgwick, it is those people
whose sexuality is said to be nonnormative who develop the
most subtle and nuanced strategies for learning how the closet
works to organize the biopower of which Foucault wrote.
Inadvertently, then, those with the less powerful position learn
how to conduct themselves—in what they say, in what they do
not say—as they navigate the often treacherous and violent
society in which they live. They become empowered *by* the
closet.

Closetedness, Sedgwick tells us, "itself is a performance
initiated as such by the speech act of a silence—not a particular
silence, but a silence that accrues particularity by fits and starts,
in relation to the discourse that surrounds and differentially
constitutes it."[12] The bind of which Foucault wrote—in
which the biopower of sexuality allows both for sexuality-as-
regulation and sexuality-as-liberation—can so subtly influence
the things that we think and say about sexuality that, as
Sedgwick points out, it gives a particular meaning to that
which in fact is *not* said or *cannot* be said.

This is what Sedgwick means by the silence that surrounds
the closet and by which she means that all sexuality—and most
importantly, queer sexuality—is informed by our knowing

what not to say and when not to say it. As Foucault wrote (and whom Sedgwick quotes), "There is no binary division to be made between what one says and what one does not say; we must try to determine the different ways of not saying such things. . . . There is not one but many silences, and they are an integral part of the strategies that underlie and permeate discourses."[13] This may sound counterintuitive to the ideas of biopower and the closet, but we should keep in mind that Foucault's theory held that all individuals—no matter how marginalized, reviled, or excluded—retain power, even if it is not to speak when they find themselves in situations that demand that they do so. Simultaneously, though, those with comparatively more power can interpret such silent acts as they might see fit, and thus for Foucault and for Sedgwick, gender and sexuality are one of the most important contexts in which social relations are negotiated and renegotiated.

Sedgwick suggests, then, that it is surprising how few actual theories and explanations we have for thinking about sexuality, given how vital it is to our understandings of ourselves and our social relations to one another. She writes, "This is among other things a way of saying that there is a large family of things *we know* and need to know about ourselves and each other with which we have, as far as I can see, so far created for ourselves almost no theoretical room to deal,"[14] and she then proposes a series of axioms, or provisional rules of study, with which we can begin to understand the roles that sexuality plays in contemporary society. There are thirteen of them, and in their substance they assert that we cannot assume that all sexual acts mean the same things to different people, nor do all people care about sexuality in the same way or even at all. For some of us, according to Sedgwick, our sexual identity matters greatly to how we define ourselves, while others among us care far more about other aspects of lives and identities. Likewise, some men and women have sexual lives that are more about their fantasies than about what they actually do, and some people fantasize about things they have no intension of acting upon. Lastly, some of us find gender difference to be key to our sexual aims and fantasies, while for others it matters less, and they are interested in a variety of different genders as part of their sexual interests.[15]

Sedgwick's axioms provide us with the tools to understand that, while sexuality sits at the heart of how we experience ourselves mentally and bodily, the particular ways in which we live our sexuality vary greatly from person to person. Remarkable about these axioms is that they hardly dwell upon many of the dominant names—"homo," "hetero," "bisexual"—which have been central to our sexual discourses. Further, the role of fantasy can both be toward acts and people we might desire or like to desire (without ever needing to act upon such desire) *and* be in aversion toward that which we do not like, approve of, or seek out for ourselves. Nevertheless, we cede importance to sexuality because it articulates something about ourselves that no other aspect of life seems able to express. In a very Foucauldian sense, sexuality as Sedgwick theorizes it here holds power over us and it concurrently is a way for us to discover how we are empowered to live more fully and creatively.

Lest we think that this way of thinking about sexuality is entirely benign or utopian, we should recall that Foucault and Sedgwick were sensitive to the fact that sexuality is quite often the arena of our political, social, and economic worlds in which we experience domination, hate, exclusion, violence, imprisonment, and death. Foucault and Sedgwick examined sexuality because it frequently is the place where we sense ourselves to be part of a larger matrix of surveillance, control, and regulation; we need only think about the energies given to debates over marriage equality, reproductive rights, transgender politics, feminism, and, not least, queer theory itself.

In another of Sedgwick's books on the topic of male same-sex desire, *Between Men: English Literature and Male Homosocial Desire*, she argues that there is a more subtle continuity between those relations between men which carry with them—either in private or in public knowledges about them—homosexual associations (i.e., an implied bodily, genital contact) as opposed to what she claimed to be a homosocial valence, in which great intimacy—emotional, intellectual, spiritual, social—is possible among men who do not think of themselves as homosexual, gay, or queer. Rather, instead of seeing these phenomena as separate, where "the homosexual" names an embodied intimacy and, by contrast, "the homosocial" implies everything else possible *except* for the sexual, genital forms of contact between men, which Sedgwick hypothesizes as "the potential unbrokenness of a continuum between homosocial and homosexual—a continuum whose visibility, for men, in our society, is radically disrupted."[16]

"Male homosocial desire" is the name that Sedgwick gives to the entire continuum of thoughts, comments, gestures, and writings—not the least, the last, because she is examining here specifically British nineteenth-century novels—which allow us to discover how inexact these names—homosexual, homosocial—are to theorize the role of sexual discourses *and* sexual acts within depictions of male-male social bonds. Further, Sedgwick's thoughts help us to understand a key distinction between desire—which she calls a structure—and love, which describes an emotion. By the former, she means a repeated social practice, which includes the telling of narratives, which ensures the continuance of privilege given to male same-sex relations across the social spectrum most often at the expense of women. Further, these male homosocial bonds take different forms for Sedgwick as they are organized by economic class and varying forms of power—Sedgwick, we should note, was deeply influenced by Foucault—that different men might share.

This portion of Sedgwick's thought might give trouble to some because she is quite consciously—from a position of seeking to defend the dignity and positive dimensions of male same-sex sexuality—establishing a continuity between men who claim themselves staunchly heterosexual and who do so by villainizing queer men and men who articulate their same-sex desire and practice as at the core of who they are. Thus, when Sedgwick provocatively writes that "when Ronald

Reagan and Jesse Helms get down to serious logrolling on 'family politics,' they are men promoting men's interests [but] is their bond in any way congruent with the bond of a loving gay male couple?" She claims that "Reagan and Helms would say no—disgustedly. Most gay couples would say no—disgustedly. But why not? Doesn't the continuum between 'men-loving-men' and 'men promoting-the-interests-of-men' have the same intuitive force that it has for women?"[17]

Feminism and queer theory

Sedgwick in the same passage quotes feminist philosopher and activist Gayle Rubin who asserts that "the suppression of the homosexual component of human sexuality, and by corollary, the suppression of homosexuals, is . . . a product of the same system whose rules and relations oppress women."[18] Yet, Sedgwick refines Rubin's insight about the oppression of homosexuals and that of women by thinking in the Foucauldian manner that homosexuality is not so much *oppressed* as it is carefully *produced* in order to substantiate and legitimate what is called heterosexuality, as that category serves to relegate both queer men and women to positions of less power. Worth noting is that these positions within Foucault's conception of power relations are hardly identical, even within themselves: women of color and working-class women share few advantages in comparison to white queer men, but the difference between white queer men working on a sheepherding operation and white queer men working employed on Wall Street is vast.

Indeed, the difference between sheepherders and bankers is the fact of labor, and the meaning of labor within the critical examination of sexuality can be discerned when we remember that queer theory developed in the legacies of feminist critique and activism, and in *Brokeback Mountain*, we discover how labor is vital to understanding the linkage between masculinity and sexuality. However, labor is also a parallel link between femininity and sexuality, and it was feminism that first offered the critical insight that gender and sexuality are the products of human work within the world.

This insight emerged because of the *lack* of remuneration of women's work—household labor, childbearing, and rearing, the care of the sick and the old—which often goes unrewarded financially and, even when it is compensated, it is done so at a much lower rate of income than that enjoyed by men. The fact that Sedgwick finds within Rubin's language the linkage between the homosocial dimensions of all men and the exclusion within patriarchy of women from positions of power tells us of the critical genealogy in which queer theory learned from and borrowed many of the most important concepts of feminism. At the same time, it is worth remembering that queer theory emerged from the need to rethink some of the most important debates within feminism about the relation of sexuality to gender, not because these debates were resolved within feminism but because they turned out to be arguments not solely about the lives of women and the political strategies that needed to be invented to address women's oppression but are a larger set of insights needed to understand how all sexuality relates to gendering.

For example, one of the central feminist debates within the period of the 1970s was the idea of how women's sexual desire is in advance politicized within patriarchy because the status of women historically has always—politically, economically, socially, intellectually—been made subordinate to men. Thus, the problem emerged within feminism about whether lesbian sexuality might be the solution for inventing new social relations of power that could develop away and apart from the world of men. In a famous series of polemic statements, some feminists argued that lesbian feminists undermined the credibility of feminism by proposing untenable ideas that failed to understand that the status of women could only be altered by direct engagement within the institutions in which women were most dominated, that is, with and by men. From the stance of lesbian feminist critique, though, this practice would, even if only inadvertently, serve to exclude lesbian sexuality from the larger social world and stigmatize it from within feminist communities.

Charactering the ideas of the latter groups of lesbian feminists, Nikki Sullivan writes that they "promoted an idealized view of female relations in which lesbians had far more in common with heterosexual women than they did with gay men" and this resulted in the fact that "gender, then, not sexuality, was seen as the basis of political coalition by activists such as these. However . . . it often seemed that to be a heterosexual women-identified woman was a contradiction in terms."[19]

In this version of feminist politics, lesbianism was both a sexual affirmation of women among themselves and a political idea that protected women from the forms of exclusion and violence that men, including gay men, benefited from imposing upon women. This "political lesbianism," as it was referred to, sought to interrogate whether all sexual acts, most centrally penetration within intercourse, was inherently political and, in its most regulatory dimensions, this feminist argument saw penetration between women as mimicking the impositions within heterosexual sex that feminism was seeking to overturn. This produced a highly polemical set of responses, not least the assertion in turn by some lesbian feminists that all sexual activity could be positive and affirming—the "sex positive" idea—and that feminism should not become the activity of proscribing what kinds of sex were associated with the best kinds of politics.

Worth recalling from these crucial debates within feminism that have shaped the problems that queer theory addresses is the idea of the essentialist gendering and sexuality of men and women. This challenging idea arose in response to the most basic of questions: What do we mean by calling someone a "man" or a "woman"—or, for that matter, a "lesbian," a "queer man," "bisexual," and so on? We might intuitively feel that we know—and that intuition is one that queer theory seeks to understand—but if we were to ask ourselves with any rigor what we mean by such terms, we would discover ourselves on difficult philosophical terrain. In the next chapter, we will examine this question at greater length through the philosophical work of Judith Butler; here I want to dwell on the essentialist idea in terms of the impact its critique had with feminism and the legacy of this critique for queer theorists.

Are we an essence of ourselves—some unchanging, immutable, version of our personality, psychology, and embodiment that, despite the outward appearance of changes, is itself an unalterable fact about us? If this were true, this aspect of us would include how we are born with biological sex and then gendered in our social lives from an early age. However, if it were the case of our essentialized sex and gender, would the category of "woman" or "man" apply in all cases where we felt it to be true—of others and of ourselves?

We can test the immense stakes involved in how we answer this question by taking into consideration two things: first, is a woman (or a man) the same individual and social being in all cases—say, from how a female-sexed child born in eleventh-century feudal France might have developed into an adult woman in her historical society to how a contemporary female-sexed child born in Haiti experiences her maturation last year? How do history, location, and social context shape the lives of such varying humans to such a degree of difference that we might realize that the name of "woman" covers an astonishing variety of different lives that it soon becomes apparent how vague, in fact, it might seem to be.

This problem became apparent for quite urgent reasons when feminist thinkers and activists in the 1970s and later queer theorists encountered strong critique from feminists of color and feminists whose economic-class identity did not coincide either with the experiences that white, comparatively privileged feminists described as part of the sexist discrimination of their lives or with the proposed solutions that might resolve such forms of discrimination. This blindness by relatively affluent feminists to the situations of other women with less power and means led to the critique of it as essentialist: that its central assumptions about which women and their forms of oppression formed the basis of political struggle were based on ideas about who counts as a woman in ways that turned out to be exclusive and myopic. The antiessentialist critique of feminism brought about a new set of feminist intellectual work and activism by writers such as Gloria Anzaldúa, Maxine Hong Kingston, Audre Lorde, and Alice Walker, and others, who thought that feminism would need to invent whole new forms of critique around the different kinds of violence and oppression which formed an aggregate of concerns but which could never resolve into a single list of such.

Second, while the examination of essentialist feminist political thought might seem to lead to greater inclusion which leads to better political and intellectual work, at its heart was a groundbreaking problem that continues to challenge us in the present moment: if one is not essentially anything—woman, lesbian, bisexual—then can one become someone else in such radical difference that our most basic notions of how we define one another are challenged in fundamental ways? One such way has emerged in debates between transgender and feminist intellectuals who see such changes in starkly different terms. Here, the challenge is to consider whether, as Simone de Beauvoir's famous assertion would have it, "One is not born but, rather becomes a woman." If that is the case, could not someone born a biologically sexed male become a woman? Do not the innovations in medical treatments—surgical, hormonal, etc.—make possible the becoming of a woman and, for that matter, becoming a man?

The contentious terms of the debate about such possibilities revolve around different ideas about how we are gendered: one emphasizes the sense that the mobility of sexual characteristics, be they breasts or chests, facial hair or smoothness, feminine gesture and masculine behavior, enable one to become another gender than one might have inherited at birth. Further, this attitude sees gender and sexuality as part of a complicated and highly varied set of possibilities by which gender, sex, and sexuality correlate with one another, such that it is possible to have individuals who self-identify in nonnormative ways with different sex-gender forms that do not resolve into male-female or masculine-feminine.

However, as some feminists would remind us, the *becoming* of a woman which Simone de Beauvoir establishes as a crucial aspect of women's experience means emerging throughout a lifetime into the socialized oppression not only of adult women, but also of infant females, girls, adolescent women; to become a woman is to know of the experience of systematized exclusion and harm toward all girls and women, albeit in different forms in different places and moments. In this frame of mind (which some have characterized as transphobic or antitransgendered feminism), becoming a woman is yet another form of patriarchal privilege where men colonize, as it were, the experiences of women and dominate them.

It was the earliest feminist philosophers, whose work in the modern period appears at the beginning of the nineteenth century, such as Mary Wollstonecraft, Flora Tristan, Elizabeth Cady Stanton, Sojourner Truth, Harriet Taylor Mill, John Stuart Mill, and Susan B. Anthony, who all emphasize four key ideas in their analyses. First, the subjection of women to men has been the historical norm in the contemporary West, as well as in many other historical periods and, second, that modernization requires a new understanding of both how women have been dominated—intellectually, physically, and emotionally—by men and how new conditions of subjugation are emerging. Third, the liberation of women from such conditions requires the examination of how all spheres of life rely upon such subjection and, four, the rejection of such violent practices and the reinvention of institutions that dominate women are central to any political project of emancipation.

The problem of labor as a political question has been central to human societies at least since the work of the philosophers G. W. F. Hegel and Karl Marx, and the particular manner in which they think about the work of men and women to survive and flourish in the world describes human societies as organized around the domination by one class of people—masters—of another class, slaves. Hegel, and subsequently Marx, would argue that it is the object of slaves to liberate themselves from the conditions of their subjection and thus slaves are engaged intellectually and physically with innovation toward that freedom in a way that no master has incentive to devise. Marx argued, as is well known, that the proletariat class of humans that developed in industrial societies after the eighteenth century would liberate themselves—and he argued, all of humanity—from the subjection of capitalist economies.

However, it was the work of the twentieth-century French philosopher Simone de Beauvoir to extend Hegel's notion of the "master-slave dialectic" to gender and sexuality and in her immensely influential book, published in 1949, *The Second Sex* (which influenced subsequent feminist thinkers, not least Betty Friedan) who saw within the theory of human history and social change offered by Hegel a way of understanding both the conditions of women's subjection and the manner in which such conditions might be altered. As a reader of Marxist philosophy, de Beauvoir was interested in how women's lives in patriarchal societies were firstly to be understood as the domination of all aspects of their lives—including their sexuality—through the labors required of them in the various institutions such as the family, schools, religion, factories, and offices. For de Beauvoir, at the heart of things was the fact that women are always laboring to produce and to reproduce, whether or not their efforts are monetarily compensated. Indeed, the fact of women's frequently failing to be monetarily compensated for such labors is at the core of de Beauvoir's analysis because she understands that those labors that are not paid distinguish women from men. Thus, no matter how meager the payment exchanged for the labor of men is, men are not expected to exert themselves for *no* wages or salary at all, while women's work often makes them reliant upon men for the resources to manage households, and bear and raise children.

Performance theory

A species that enslaves the female punishes the male
attempting to escape: it eliminates him brutally.

—SIMONE DE BEAUVOIR[20]

One of the most important ways of thinking about gender,
sex, and sexuality that develops within Foucault's theories is
how the ways in which we think and act upon our sexuality
are always simultaneously both highly liberatory—or, at least,
contain the possibilities of liberation—and highly regulatory.
By this, Foucault meant that the way sexuality and power are
linked in modern societies suggests that those whose sexuality
is affected by institutions that lay claim to knowledge about
such matters—that would be virtually everyone—seek to push
against the boundaries of what is seen as normal and to claim
their sexuality as an aspect of their life in which they seek
to express their freedom. That is all well and good until we
realize that this tends to confirm the very structures of power
that organize and hold sway over what forms of sexuality are
allowable and which are not.

   This densely co-constituted relation between the liberatory
and the regulatory shapes the foundational work of the feminist
American philosopher Judith Butler as she has built upon the
work of Foucault but as well reminds us that feminist critiques
by Simone de Beauvoir, Monique Wittig, Luce Irigaray, and
Gayle Rubin are necessary for understanding how sexuality
and gender shape the experiences—not least, of power—of
women and queer people in a heteronormative and patriarchal
society. Butler's work in the arena of performance theory has
had widespread influence over the work of philosophers,
sociologists and anthropologists, literary scholars, and, as the
name suggests, historians of media and performance studies.

   At the heart of Butler's arguments about gender and
sexuality resides an immense reversal of our expectations
about how we typically have thought about the relation of

sexuality to gender and it is worth taking time to understand her critique and the basis on which she organizes it. She begins with the key assertion, made by the French feminist Simone de Beauvoir, "One is not born a woman, but rather becomes one." Butler notices in de Beauvoir's claim the idea that sex or gender is not contained within an individual woman as a static entity that is something that an infant would be born with— but instead is something that one becomes over time, and if the status of *being* a woman is defined as *becoming* that very thing—a woman—then how might we ever be able to define what it is that constitutes a woman? What moment among the stages in which something develops do we seize upon as *the* defining moment?

Through an extended analysis of the various roles that human females are expected to perform within patriarchal societies—girl, married woman, mother, lesbian, and prostitute—de Beauvoir points to our significant inability to define exactly what a woman is and asserts that there is no positive definition available. Instead, a woman is understood as a negation to what constitutes the life of men: men exist and can act, but women are always approaching a horizon of becoming, maintaining the possibility of emerging as a social being whose actions are meaningful and can shape the world, but not having yet achieved that role. As Butler comments about de Beauvoir's critique, "If there is something right in Beauvoir's claim that one is not born, but rather *becomes* a woman, it follows that *woman* itself is a term in process, a becoming, a constructing that cannot rightfully be said to originate or to end."[21]

While de Beauvoir argues that a woman is not a positive, definable entity, Butler's philosophy does not remain content with this insight and Butler extends de Beauvoir's central assertion about the status of women to consider how *all* sex and gendering of humans is impossible to define in such terms—that is, to understand as an essence or to *essentialize*. Butler radically insists that the idea that anyone has a stable and unchanging, knowable and consistent essence for living within one's sexuality and one's gendering is a fiction, although it is a necessary fiction for the social order to be preserved. In this regard, Butler agrees with Foucault on how sexuality and power are intertwined and cannot be parted one from another.

That said, we should at this point clarify some of the key terms which de Beauvoir and Butler are interrogating, most notably sex, sexuality, and gender, because each of these will be revealed by these feminist critiques—critiques that form the basis for much of queer theory—as highly ideological and hardly "natural" in any sense.

Sex, as commonly used in the biological sciences, refers to the manner in which organisms are physiologically organized to reproduce through the differentiation between female and male anatomical configuration, with some individual humans—those who are intersexed—bearing anatomical traits of both sexes. The biological sexual distinctions drawn between female and male humans historically have included chromosomes, reproductive organs, and secondary sexual characteristics which are ascertained as either female or male. These categories of male and female are necessary as the basis for reproduction of the human species.

We can gain a sense of the importance of biological sex distinctions for the gendering of humans when we consider the first social name assigned to all humans upon birth, and with medical imaging technologies, now within the womb, as either female or male. The regulatory functions of the state and the hospital immediately enact their power over the sexing of humans when the birth certificate demands the entering of one of these names for recording the fact of the birth, and the assignment of the sex category as either male or female will follow us for the rest of our lives, on school registrations, driver's licenses, passports, and all manner of documentation that seeks to gather data about human populations.

Sex as a category that derives from medical and scientific exploration does not necessarily tell us how we as humans act upon each other socially with the bodies that we inhabit, any more than needing to eat can tell us how and why we raise plants and livestock in order to cook or about the pleasures that we derive from food and its many cultural inflections. While we may indeed often derive pleasure from the many practices which our sexed bodies offer to us, the immense variety of how we live our sexed bodies provides us the opportunity to see how variation is expressed culturally. Further, being born with a sexed body does not entail automatically that one will have conventional, if not compulsory, forms of desire and pleasure that somehow conform between biology and culture. To be born female, as de Beauvoir repeatedly asserts, does not presume that one will want to marry, to have sexual contact with men, to bear or nurture children. The fact of this noncoincidence is the difference between sex and the experience of the sexed body within society.

Gender is how a culture conventionally expects an individual to express, through dress, gesture, deportment, behaviors, and attitudes, the fact of their biological sex. While the categories of male and female are categories of sex distinction, masculinity and femininity are related to how humans are gendered, and in the most conventional ideas about the relation of gender to sex, often masculinity is associated with males while femininity is associated with females. This again is the difference between sex as biological category and gender as cultural practice.

The fact that a given culture might have multiple notions of appropriate masculinities and femininities which form the basis for social recognition and validation of males and females, respectively, tells us that there is hardly even a singular category of masculinity or femininity operative within any given society, so that it is possible for a working-class woman in contemporary France to have her experience of her sexual assignment as female shaped by very different gendered expectations for a more privileged woman, while her counterpart in the United States, in China, or in Chile, might have very different gendered expectations of her. Further, gender roles can and do change over the course of time, making them *historical*—what a women within the racial and class situation of her moment might be expected to say, wear, or do in the 1950s is highly different than what would be or was expected of her in the present moment or two centuries ago.

The expression of sex through gender is further complicated by the fact of *sexuality*, which comprises those thoughts, feelings, bodily sensations, and forms of contact with others that have been, as we have seen, part of the regulatory naming project of sexology, with the categories of "homosexual," "heterosexual," "bisexual," and others emerging to describe the ostensible categories of sexual relations among men and women. The relations between sex, gender, and sexuality sit at the center of sexology's concerns with the sexual aim of a given man or woman—say, to have sexual contact with another man or another woman—occupying the taxonomic project of psychiatry, psychology, medicine, biology, and social sciences.

An important recent distinction that has arisen in order to draw attention to differences between sex, gender, and sexuality is that of identifying as either cis- or as trans- with the two prefixes intended to call attention to the disjunction between sex and gender. A cis-gender male is someone who at birth is identified with male sexual characteristics and whose gendering aligns with the expectations that he appear and behave in typical fashion, that is, he be masculine. A trans-male may be born as a biological female but who comports herself through the terms of femininity; she may choose to employ different hormonal or surgical treatments to alter her body to appear as such, or she may not.

We should wonder about whether the conventional ideas we have inherited about sex, gender, and sexuality are explanations that liberate sexual possibility or, as Foucault and Butler would insist, regulate and constrain us. Put another way, do we risk ignoring multiple, varied, and undisclosed relations among these three categories because we might, in point of fact, discover that they operate by silencing those sexualities that don't neatly find their place within the terms on offer?

Butler argues that a queer feminist critique of gender that is informed by the insights of de Beauvoir and Foucault would need to see the exclusions made necessary for patriarchal sexological understanding to operate and to consider them as that: a necessity for the power operations that exclude and harm women and queer people. She writes that "the law produces and then conceals the notion of 'a subject before the law' in order to invoke that discursive foundation as a naturalized foundational premise that subsequently legitimates that law's own regulatory hegemony."[22] Butler takes aim at the idea that all forms of sexuality are said to be represented in the regulatory regimes that have power over individuals within them, and she wonders about the kinds of sexuality whose exclusion bolsters that same power. If the naming of kinds of sexuality in point of fact validates them, then it is worth wondering about those other sexualities that are strategically omitted or ignored because there may be advantage to those agents and institutions that claim power over sexuality in what is ignored or excluded by them. Even more to the point, the greatest advantage might be gained over those sexualities and genderings that are most excluded from the domain of power.

In this regard, Butler is pressing at the limits of Foucault's critique of the repressive hypothesis in that, while her analysis concurs with Foucault's sense of how power and knowledge align, it remains the case that so much of what is regulated by the power/knowledge dynamic, for Butler, is also what remains silent and unarticulated within it. On the one hand, thus, she writes about Foucault's theory that "the object of repression is not *the desire* it takes to be its ostensible object, but the multiple configurations of power itself . . . desire and its repression are an occasion for the consolidation of juridical structures."

Simultaneously, for Butler, something is still left out of this account because the repressive hypothesis maintains that *only* those forms of sexual practice that are produced through their repression are recognizable for regulatory institutions. Are there sexualities that might exist externally to those institutions? For Butler, the answer to this question appears within the way that de Beauvoir's account of how the differences between men and women—the difference between being and becoming—have relegated women's sexuality and women's gendering to a non-status that would seem to evade the ideas that Foucault offers. While Foucault's theories help significantly to explain how sexuality has been regulated in the modern era, the meanings of gender as they relate to sexual difference receive less attention within Foucault's account and, insightful as Foucault's intellectual work is, his work attended little to the concerns of feminism.

Subsequent queer feminist critiques, on the other hand, address the conditions of women's and queer people's lives in societies in which the bulk of power, status, and wealth are given to straight-identified men, and thus the nature of *gendered* difference becomes urgent for understanding how sexual difference is a field of power and discrimination which queer theory seeks to dismantle. Queer theorists have learned much from feminist intellectual and activist work, not least Butler's, because feminism has developed powerful critiques for theorizing gendered power.

That said, how does gender difference enforce relations of power? Butler argues that the concept of gender is based on the performance of an ideal which in point of fact does not exist and which no one in fact ever achieves in absolute fashion. Gender—understood as the social practices that express ideas of sexual difference, both in terms of biological sex differentiation and in terms of the ways in which we talk about sexual aims and sexual goals (the language of "heterosexual" "homosexual," and "bisexual")—contains within it the notion of a stable category which we would be at pains to discover either individually or socially among us.

As Butler comments, "*gender* is not a noun," and by this she means that it does not exist for our social lives as a thing, but instead is a process and set of ideas that we practice, all the while behaving as if gender were in fact a noun, a thing that exists and which one can become. The difference between those two aspects of gender—that it is not a thing but an idea, and yet our actions and thoughts enforce it as if it were a thing—lies at the heart of how gender is a form of politics in the way that Butler's critique sees it. At the same time, Butler argues that gender is not "a set of free-floating attributes, for the substantive effect of gender is performatively produced and compelled by the regulatory practices of gender coherence." While there is a liberatory possibility contained within the insight that gender is not a noun, the insistence on what Butler calls "gender coherence" makes the practice of gender one of the densest sites of power within our culture.

Yet, Butler's goal is not solely to tell us that gender is another form of what Foucault would call power, but instead to ask how we might begin to seek justice in the face of domination where there are always hazards to being named as perverse. This is what Butler means by "representation," and her work questions whether it is an effective political strategy—for feminists or for queer theorists and activists—solely to seek inclusion on a roster of identities. To be represented for her is to be encompassed within preexisting power relations; as she asks, "What relations of domination and exclusion are inadvertently sustained when representation becomes the sole focus of politics?"[23]

The critique of gender through the perception that it is performative (i.e., not a noun, but a practice) heralds a different approach and one which she rightly sees as having been offered by de Beauvoir's writings. But, what does it mean to say that gender is performative? And, if it is, how so?

Gender is performative because of two primary characteristics: it *performs* power and it does so *by repetition*. As regards the first aspect, gender gains us social recognition when it most conforms to internalized expectations in order to allow us to speak and to act; that is, to have power. Butler sees the performance of gender as demanding of us that we enact socially sanctioned ideals of how our gender corresponds (ostensibly) with our sex, and the significant insight she offers about this relation between gender and sex is that our thinking about them is based on questionable assumptions about sex as being unchanging in the ways that we think about it. Our ideas about the "nature" of the body as solely biologically given are what we, in the contemporary era, think are the basis or ground of gender, but Butler sees this as the manner in which our cultural assumptions about science (i.e., especially sexology) bolster rather than question whether there need be—indeed, whether there can be—any biological basis for how we live our gendered selves. As Butler comments, "[The] production of sex as the prediscursive ought to be understood as the effect of the apparatus of cultural construction designated by gender."[24]

The effect of the reversal which Butler has in mind about her misgivings of seeing sex as the biological basis for gender performance is to understand that there is little reason to assume that the many forms that gender takes hardly point to our being sexed as male or female. Gender is not a binary. Indeed, such assumptions obscure the fact that we cannot with any rigor assume any causation between sex and gender except that which, in Butler's terms, we enact.

However, we risk much when we test in any way the alleged correspondence between sex and gender because the rupture between them within gender performance is so fraught. What keeps us from questioning the specious relation between sex and gender is its repetition—indeed, the demand for repetition—of gendered performative gestures that code as masculine or feminine. But, with every repetition comes difference because no gesture is identical with the prior one, and indeed each installment points to variation in the sequence. Thus, we might look to the forms of masculine and feminine performance in popular culture as clues about the weak determination between sex and gender. It is probably no accident that films that test this assumption gather as much attention as they do because they display quite vividly gender-as-performance.

Yet, if we extend the critique of gendered performance to other aspects of contemporary social life, we discover unexpected dimensions of identity that bear hallmarks in the way we think about them that are similar to gender and sexuality.

We can begin with race. It might seem an obvious aspect of the film's fictional world that it has been populated largely by white Americans, but what in actual fact does that mean, and how does the film enact a particular version of whiteness? While recognizing that the world of rural Wyoming ranching and sheepherding in the 1960s probably constituted a human population of many white-identified men and women, we should ask about the fact of the film's exclusions: Why is there no sense of the American Indian, among whose tribes prior to European colonization included Arapaho, Bannock, Cheyenne, Comanche, Crow, Dakota Sioux, Kiowa, Pawnee, Shoshone, and the Ute? Does the west of this Western include the Latino and Chicano worlds, or other non-northern European colonists who inhabit the space? We witness brief exchanges between other laborers who are referred to as Portuguese, but that designation is unclear as to whether it confirms men of Portuguese heritage or whether it is some racial shorthand that white men such as Ennis and Jack employ to encompass vaguely a range of ethnic or racial identities.

These questions are not intended solely to evaluate the film's racial depictions in a simplistic ethical manner, where we might too easily castigate it as needing some more complicated racial tableaux to confirm our sense of the complexity of the social world the film is depicting; nor should we seek inclusive representations of racial difference which might distort our sense—one that is rightful—of comparative racial stratification in the historical era in which the film is set.

Instead, asking the question of whiteness is a way of gaining a sense of the film's performances as marked by assumptions—racial assumptions—that we would benefit from having made apparent for us. Richard Dyer puts it best when he reminds us that "since race in itself—insofar as it is anything in itself—refers to some intrinsically insignificant geographical/physical differences between people, it is the imagery of race that is in play"[25] in much of contemporary life. Dyer's work on whiteness insists on offering us a strong reminder that, if race is a way of thinking about differences among humans, then one of the most powerful ideological effects of the status given to whites is to obscure the fact that whiteness is a race as much as any other. Drawing on the work of bell hooks, Hazel Carby, and other historians and theorists of race, Dyer notes that whiteness gains much of its privilege by seeming to be nonracial; it is an unmarked race, whereas all others are marked as races. He writes: "To say that one is interested in race has come to mean that one is interested in any racial imagery other than that of white people. Yet, race is not only attributable to people who are not white, nor is imagery of nonwhite people the only racial imagery."

To fail seeing the whiteness of a character as that character is performed in a film serves to preserve in unquestioned fashion this status because, as Dyer (who is white and British) tells us, "As long as race is something only applied to nonwhite peoples, as long as white people are not racially seen and named, they/we function as a human norm."

If we need any additional encouragement to bring the racial dimensions into the foreground for us, we might ask what the effect of having Ennis and Jake played by Chicano, Japanese-American, or African American actors would be upon the spectator. We would probably immediately feel compelled to note this feature of the characters and to speculate strongly upon the meaning of this casting decision for our interpretation of the narrative. So, too, should we with the whiteness of the film's characters.

In this regard, our reading of the film extends Butler's critique of gender to understand that, like gender, race is "an historical situation rather than a natural fact." Race, too, in similar but not identical fashion needs to be understood as a historical situation rather than a fact of nature. Thus we can ask: What kinds of white people are these men and women? What is the historical situation of the whiteness of Ennis, Jack, Alma, and Lureen? If their situation is one in which their bodies, as male- and female-sexed bodies, are white bodies, how do they maintain their identities through race as much as through their gender in what Butler calls "a sustained and repeated corporeal project"?

For one thing, they need to work and are reduced for the most part to manual labor in order to subsist (the exception arising when Lureen begins to ascend within her father's business to the management of the company). The fact that Ennis in particular seems unable to move beyond the subsistence made possible by the punishing physical labor demanded by his work on ranches draws our attention to one of the more glaring contradictions within the myth of the Western cowboy, a myth that gender performance serves to ameliorate: that it seems there are few opportunities to rise through any reward structure out and away from this base labor. If we nurture a fantasy of cowboy masculinity that it is its own reward, then we should ask ourselves how it might ever move beyond its own conditions for being at the most basic level of seeking social mobility (another cherished value of American masculinity).

How, we might ask, is this a function of race as performance within the film and within the Western's idealization of the west? For one thing, we might ask ourselves how the whiteness of cowboys allows them to achieve an identity within their labor which paradoxically makes them heroic in a way in which, were we to substitute a different race or ethnicity within the casting, we would discover the lack of historical referents to confirm such heroism. It is not a coincidence that the hagiography of cowboy masculinity within the film Western includes almost solely white men, and the repetitive function of performance relies upon such historical precedent through which to make sense of gendered and racialized enactments.

Gwendolyn Audrey Foster takes up this contradictory status of white masculine performance in the history of the Western by describing the history of white performance in the film Western as both naturalized and artificial. Drawing attention to the fact of "gluelike white face paint" which early film actors wore in order to underscore the pale quality of their skin, and the ongoing practice of making up performers to appear, as she puts it, "whiter than white" on film and on video, she offers the insight that we might become sensitized to how racialized performance (via makeup and lighting) is underscored in ways that gender performance seems even more naturalized. She quotes Dyer on whiteness, who offers that "race and gender are ineluctably intertwined, through the primacy of heterosexuality in reproducing the former and defining the latter. It is a productively unstable alliance."[26] Dyer and Foster draw our attention to the way in which dominant categories of race and gender—here, whiteness and heteronormativity—are bound up one within the other, and while our critical attentions may focus upon one or the other, we are better served to attempt seeing them as co-constituting.

Eve Sedgwick offered that this performative dimension of texts can participate in what she calls the hermeneutics of suspicion and paranoia, where the discovery of the racist, homophobic, and misogynist aspects of a social practice or a representation is thought to be sufficient to generate some kind of benefit from that insight. Sedgwick's sense of how this paranoid critical work—which as a foundational figure in queer theory she admitted to in her own earlier criticism—needed to be attuned to other possibilities which the "paranoid" critical practice often seemed to exclude or deride.[27] She writes that

> only [queer theory's] cruel and contemptuous assumption that the one thing lacking for global revolution, explosion of gender roles, or whatever, is people's (that is, other people's) having the painful effects of their oppression, poverty, or deludedness sufficiently exacerbated to make the pain conscious (as if otherwise it wouldn't have been) and intolerable (as if intolerable situations were famous for generating excellent solutions.)[28]

Sedgwick here is calling to account how much queer theory loses its effect when it sees itself as remote from the conditions of everyday life and somehow able to understand the experiences of oppressed LGBQT people better than they can. In this regard, her insights and own astonishing critical work return queer theory to a place in which it started—with the sense of urgency about the manner in which sexuality and gender are risk-filled dimensions of life—and to a maturity in which the enterprise can allow for other modes of thought in addition to that of the paranoid.

Another mode that Sedgwick had in mind in the work she published before her death in 2009 is what she called the reparative. The paranoid queer critical position seeks to be prepared for all dismal outcomes, which is warranted if we recall the ongoing assaults against queers, but it also claims to know all the possibilities of only negative outcomes. For Sedgwick, it leaves out the possibility of any forms of positive affect: of pleasure not taken in the grim knowledge of how queer people are hurt, but pleasure taken in the pleasure of being, well, queer. Such reparative queer theory, as distinct from its paranoid cousin, surrenders knowing in advance all outcomes in exchange for admitting that some things cannot and need not be known about queer life and queer history in advance. Sedgwick writes, "To read from a reparative position is to surrender the knowing, anxious paranoid determination that no horror, however apparently unthinkable, shall ever come to the reader *as new*." In her understanding, "To a reparatively positioned reader, it can seem realistic and necessary to experience surprise. Because there can be terrible surprises, however there can also be good ones."[29]

Remarkable about the legacy of an earlier moment in the unfolding forms of thought within queer theory is that if the traumas are responded to quickly, they can seem to repeat themselves ad infinitum, begging the question for Sedgwick: Will queer theory solely attend itself to those traumas? This is not to deny the validity and intensity of such experiences as they are experienced by LGBQT people, but rather to wonder if anything else is possible.

The theory of performance as queer critique of gender and sexuality considers how we are enacting Foucault's liberatory/regulatory rules. It allows for us to discover how varied and different cultural actors, including makers and audiences of cinema, reshape—that is, perform—versions of themselves, of culture, of politics, that help them to live. In this sense, performance theory is much like a performance: it demands that we see both the illusory aspects of gender (much as we would understand a stage play to be a fiction) while knowing that performance has powerful effects (we would take from a well-staged play that moved us much to remember and to consider in the performance's aftermath). Butler tells us that "to claim that gender is constructed is not to assert its illusoriness or artificiality, where those terms are understood to reside within a binary that counterposes the 'real' and the 'authentic' as oppositional."

As we will discover in the next chapter, the critiques at hand—from de Beauvoir, Foucault, Sedgwick, Butler—are not solely about the insights they provide about the way we live our everyday lives (although they are very much about that) but can expand our critical understanding of how an immensely popular and widely screened film such as *Brokeback Mountain* concerns itself with these questions as well.

Notes

1 Michel Foucault, *The History of Sexuality, Volume One*, trans. Robert Hurley (New York: Vintage Books, 1978), 158.

2 Nikki Sullivan, *A Critical Introduction to Queer Theory* (New York: New York University Press, 2003), 1.

3 Foucault, *The History of Sexuality*, 37.

4 Ibid., 60.

5 Ibid., 63.

6 Ibid., 94–95.

7 Ibid., 159.

8 Judith Butler, *Gender Trouble: Feminism and the Subversion of Identity* (New York: Routledge, 1999), 4.

9 Annamarie Jagose, *Queer Theory: An Introduction* (New York: New York University Press, 1996), 81.

10 Jagose, *Queer Theory*, 11.

11 Eve Kosofsky Sedgwick, *Epistemology of the Closet* (Berkeley: University of California Press, 1990), 1.

12 Sedgwick, *Epistemology*, 3.

13 Foucault, *The History of Sexuality*, 27.

14 Sedgwick, *Epistemology*, 24.

15 Ibid., 25–26.

16 Eve Kosofsky Sedgwick, *Between Men: English Literature and Male Homosocial Desire* (New York: Columbia University Press, 1985), 1–2.

17 Sedgwick, *Between Men*, 3.

18 Gayle Rubin, "The Traffic in Women: Notes Toward a Political Economy of Sex," in *Toward an Anthropology of Women*, ed. Rayna Reiter (New York: Monthly Review Press, 1975), 180.

19 Sullivan, *Queer Theory*, 33.

20 Simone de Beauvoir, *The Second Sex*, trans. Constance Borde and Sheila Malovany-Chevallier (New York: Vintage Books, 2011), 33.

21 Judith Butler, *Gender Trouble: Feminism and the Subversion of Identity* (New York: Routledge, 1990), 43.

22 Butler, *Gender Trouble*, 5.

23 Ibid., 9.

24 Ibid.,11.

25 Richard Dyer, "The Matter of Whiteness," in *White Privilege: Essential readings on the Other Side of Racism*, ed. Paula S. Rothenberg (New York: Worth Publishers, 2005), 11.

26 Dyer, *White Privilege*, 30.

27 Sedgwick was not diagnosing individual critics, but rather describing a frame of mind which she saw as nearly inevitable for queer theory, at least in its earliest stages.

28 Eve Kosofsky Sedgwick, *Touching Feeling: Affect, Pedagogy, Performativity* (Durham: Duke University Press, 2003), 144.

29 Sedgwick, *Touching Feeling*, 146.

CHAPTER TWO

Queer theory and *Brokeback Mountain*

Biopolitics in *Brokeback Mountain*

The conceptual tools of queer theory are expansive in their ability to analyze and understand gender and sexuality more generally, but we can now turn to the specific text of *Brokeback Mountain* in order to understand how to interpret a film through the terms at hand. Lee's film offers an opening for us to consider how queer theory would make sense of the narrative of Ennis del Mar and Jack Twist's lifelong bond.

Recalling psychoanalysis' insistence that gender and sexuality are shaped from the earliest moments in life and the manner in which we recall such experiences as they shape us, we should consider the moment in the film in which Ennis describes to Jack a childhood experience in which he accompanied his father to look upon the dead body of a neighboring rancher; this neighbor was rumored to be part of a same-sex couple and was tortured and murdered for that perception. There are many possible explanations in the larger narrative for Ennis' apparent fear over any discovery of his relations to Jack, which results in his refusal to engage Jack in anything beyond their annual shared time in the mountains. A psychoanalytic interpretation of this portion of the film would consider how the two are related: childhood trauma sponsors a lifelong avoidance of the recurrence of a painful memory, even if the avoidance ultimately brings about more suffering than the memory itself. The film organizes this moment in a flashback sequence in which the young Ennis, his father, and his brother seek out the corpse in order to bear witness to the stakes of queer sexuality, and the fact that this is visually registered within the film—not simply reported by Ennis in conversation, but filmed—connects the moment to Ennis' sense of himself as someone who should loath and avoid any possible sexual contact with another male. In order to connect the event with the feeling, though, he must, in the terms of psychoanalysis and Foucault's critique of it, confess the residing potency of the memory for him.

This is part of a larger pattern of confession by Ennis which forms the basis of his connection to Jack. Elsewhere, in Ennis' first speech in the film to Jack at the campfire, he describes his childhood and adolescence, the loss of his parents, his need to work, his intention to marry Alma, all a confession, and when Jack tells him that this is more he has heard from Ennis in two weeks and Ennis remarks that this is more than he has ever said, the conjunction of confessional speaking to erotics becomes apparent. Foucault would see Ennis' confession here as a prologue to sexual contact and not solely as coincidence: one must divulge a part of one's interior life in order to gain access to one's own bodily pleasures.

Here, we can discern Foucault's notion of biopolitics at work, a notion that always begins with questions of power: Who are these men and women and how does the biopolitics of the mid-twentieth-century rural American west define them? Are there even names for who they are and for their sexualities? In the spirit of Sedgwick's technique of stating what might seem obvious but unsaid, they are working class, white, and part of a world that compels these characters toward the drudgery of work, both that paid for and that not. The narrative begins with a conversation about labor: Ennis and Jack apply for jobs tending to sheep on a mountain in Wyoming, where they are reduced to the barest of circumstances, sleeping in tents, eating mostly prepared food, eking out a small wage by performing the job of protecting the herd of sheep from predators. While the appeal of doing such might appeal to us because of the natural grandeur and beauty of the American western mountains and the related mythology of the cowboy's autonomy and freedom, we should not neglect that the characters have minimal education and few employment prospects. They have not chosen this life so much as it is the sole life available to them and, if our capacity to labor and by implication to earn a living is the basis on which our lives are predicated, their labor is hardly more than what a well-trained herding dog might perform.

This last point is not meant dismissively but is offered as a way of understanding how very much these men are reduced to a living made possible by their functioning through their bodies: their capacity to move, to see and hear, to live and sleep under hostile physical conditions and weather; thus the biopolitics of Ennis and Jack is one in which they have little power and which power stems from their being able to rely upon (seemingly) only their most basic of physical functioning. Indeed, the arrogant and dismissive attitude of their boss toward them underscores how very much their livelihood is at the bottom of the class hierarchy of their world. Put most bluntly, the sheep that they protect have probably as much value as they do. Ennis del Mar and Jack Twist have biopolitics barely above farm animals.

In this context, their reduction to the bare life of animal dwelling within nature paradoxically provides them with the opportunity to become something entirely self-fashioned through the discovery of their shared erotic life. In this regard, the film tells us about how even the most discounted of us bears the possibility of changing into someone new through our sexuality. In Foucault's terms, there is little regulation or biopower naming of sexuality in the rural world that they inhabit and this makes it possible for them to invent a bond which might previously have seemed impossible and which, upon its subsequent discovery by others, is held to be shocking for making them into something—men having sex with each other—which no one seems to have deemed likely to happen. This is no small point: while we should remember that the historical period in which the narrative unfolds vilified sex between men, it is not the case in which at the outset this was explicitly prohibited or denied to them.

This is where the organizing silences of which Foucault wrote come to bear upon our understanding of the film: on the one hand, no one had to tell Ennis and Jack that they should not seek sexual contact with each other because there was a tacit understanding in this historical moment that this was prohibited, but, on the other hand, the failure to express this leaves open their sexual exploration because no such exclusion was ever made explicit, although Ennis certainly bears the childhood memory of how men suspected of having sexual and romantic relations were violently dealt with. The emphasis here is upon how sexuality can develop as much in the conditions of silence and non-naming as much as it can in the speech-acts of articulating our desires and pleasures in the name of a designated social role of "the homosexual" or "the heterosexual" man or woman.

Sedgwick's notion of the closet becomes instructive here because of its significant absence within *Brokeback Mountain*; that is, there is no closet out of which these characters emerge in order to find the ostensible liberations of "coming out." The concept of the closet came to the center of gay/lesbian identity politics in the 1970s as a technique through which to alter the power relations of sexuality through acts of self-naming, but it is hardly the case that such forms of self-proclamation are the sole manner in which languages, bodies, and desires can be conjoined.

In Sedgwick's terms, the homosocial bond between Ennis and Jack—but others as well within the masculine bonds of men within the film—is legible to the social world within the film because it is acceptable for men in such conditions—the rural American west—to spend large amounts of time solely within the company of men *without* an apparent possibility that such single-sex social spaces might contain within them the possibility of producing same-sex sexuality. However, it is important to note that such a possibility is realized for the two central male figures *and* for the viewer, and part of the film's appeal, I would argue, is that this shared knowledge between text and audience allows viewers such as ourselves who live within a world that defines sexual knowledge through Sedgwick's notion of the epistemology of the closet another a very different way of seeing a relation between sexual knowledge and power, one where its very hiddenness—as opposed to its disclosure—is the source of its meaning. Put another way, we who have inherited the repressive hypothesis and Sedgwick's epistemology are intrigued to consider how nondisclosure awards power to Ennis and Jack. Over the years of the narrative, they can continue to return to the mountain because they do not articulate their pleasure other than to each other.

The impact of this undisclosed aspect of their relationship is most intensely felt, aside from the two men, by their wives, Alma and Lureen, and while it might be tempting to see these characters as ancillary to *Brokeback Mountain*, the relation of queer theory to feminist critique as discussed above can show us how much these two women's experiences—while depicted in briefer fashion—are central to how the film is asking us to think about gender and sexuality. A few things about Alma and Lureen are worth noting in this regard. First, they are each depicted as sexually curious, playful, and engaged, a point worth noting in terms of how the relations they have with their husbands are not about them being unavailable or rejecting of sexual pleasure within their marriages. Second, they labor both within their households as well as in the larger workforce: Alma has a job in the supermarket, while Lureen manages the financial accounts at her father's business. Third, they are raising children—Alma and Ennis have two daughters, while Lureen and Jack have a son—and their roles as mothers are underscored in the film as being affected by their husbands' time away from their homes.

These three aspects of Alma del Mar and Lureen Twist can begin to organize a feminist reading of *Brokeback Mountain*, which would emphasize the manner in which the lives of these two women are very much dependent upon the men whom they marry, and while the film's narrative most centrally dwells upon the bond between the two men, the two women's presence deserves our critical and theoretical scrutiny.

The need for this scrutiny emerges from the fact that queer theory's debt to feminism reminds us not only that many of the primary critical techniques of queer theory are inheritances from feminism but as well we should emphasize the effect that Ennis and Jack's lives have on those who, in fact, have even fewer forms of social or economic mobility or enhancement: their wives. If the prospects of the uneducated male menial laborer in the period depicted in the film is restricted to bare subsistence, then the opportunities afforded to the women married to them offer even fewer chances. (Lureen is the exception here by dint of family and, in turn, her education.) This allows us to understand a long-standing concern within feminism which is strongly echoed within the work of Foucault and others after him: the relation between sex/gender and economic class.

Thus, the status of women within *Brokeback Mountain* is not marginal or supplemental to the narrative of the men's lives but in fact crucial for it, not least if we understand that the relative leisure and mobility afforded to Jack and Ennis derives in so many instances in this film from their wives' ability and (qualified) willingness to support them as they spend time together over the decades of their relationship. When Alma mentions in the heat of an argument that, after many seasons of his annual fishing trips with Jack, she looked inside his fishing creel only to discover that he had never in fact used it—that is, his fishing trips involved no apparent fishing—her indignation and anger might stem in part from the requirement that she labor at her supermarket job in order for him to travel with Jack. The fact of her suspicion that there was a "perverse" sexual relation between the two of them only intensifies her resentment toward the situation, but at the heart of things is that Ennis' freedom to be with Jack on the occasions in which they returned to the mountains was made possible by Alma's and Lureen's labors.

In this regard, *Brokeback Mountain* warrants feminist critiques that historicize this idealized version of life in the post–Second World War United States before the effects of feminist activism could make apparent the exploitation of women for the well-being of men. Worth recalling is that Betty Friedan's *The Feminine Mystique*—the book credited by many with the reanimation of feminist thought and activism after the quiescent decades in the mid-twentieth-century period— was published in 1963, the moment in which *Brokeback Mountain* begins, and it seems no small coincidence that the film's speculative fantasy about the men's shared life comes at the expense of the women who would benefit from the insights that Friedan and subsequent feminist thinkers would offer. For the purposes of our inquiry into *Brokeback Mountain*, then, we can gather the insights of US feminist thought around two primary problems for understanding the subjection of women: labor and sexuality.

Recalling Simone de Beauvoir's claim that women are constantly laboring—performing—to become themselves, here we should note that the women in *Brokeback Mountain* work to enable the pleasures—both known and furtive—which the men are able to enjoy. In this regard, though, there are important differences between Alma and Lureen in most aspects of their characterization. Alma is plain, shy, and works at a grocery store, while Lureen is pretty, gregarious, rides competitive show horses, and subsequently has an important role in her father's tractor dealership, suggesting that her university education has made possible a life that remains remote to Alma. In parallel key scenes in which we see them in relation to their husbands, we discover them in workplaces; when Ennis brings his baby daughter to Alma as she works in the supermarket in order to travel for his work, we discover the conflation of her unwaged labor as a mother with the waged labor she performs at the market. Ennis is oblivious to the imposition of leaving their daughter (with no notice) with Alma because, paradoxically, her maternal role is always taken as given: it can be assumed that it supersedes her capacity to serve as breadwinner for the family. At the same time, by implication he can denigrate her paid work because it is supplemental to his work on the ranch, meaning that his labor is more highly prized than hers.

Lureen, in strong contrast, enjoys a greater freedom and greater reward for her work at the tractor dealership and in the sequence in which she and Jack converse in her office regarding a lost jacket he seeks to take on a trip with Ennis, the mise-en-scène positions her as the more significant source of income for this household to the point that Jack is infantilized in their marriage. Lureen treats Jack as another child and when, subsequently, during a conversation with Ennis, Jack asserts that his father-in-law would probably be willing to pay him off to leave his marriage, he equates this subordinate status with that of being more of an employee within his marriage than a husband. Worth noting is that Ennis rebuffs him—he is taking care of his daughters that weekend and cannot spend time with Jack; we then see Jack's departure in which he weeps as he drives away. The strong combination of elements within Jack's character relate several key things to note as part of a feminist/queer critique of the film: that Jack is a child, an employee, and, not least, quite feminized in the characterization of him as capable of emotional expression where Ennis' western masculinity seems not. In this regard, the juncture between gender and economic class within the film emerges as important for our understanding of how the film is articulating a relation between the economic dimensions and the gendered sexual experiences of its characters' lives.

The relation of sex/gender to class within the film plays out within the art direction itself, with Alma and Ennis' domestic life together photographed in dimly lighted washed-out grays and browns, an aesthetic that underscores the impoverishment of their lives and the bleakness of their prospects. Their apartment above a laundromat in the small town in which they live is furnished with the necessities but not much else beyond that. By contrast, the film's visual organization of Jack and Lureen's home-life is one of brightly lighted mid-twentieth-century consumerism and comparative economic prosperity, with large new televisions and electronic gadgets—the electric knife at the Thanksgiving table signals much—a hallmark of the idealized world of middle-class Americans in the 1960s and 1970s. These visual elements help us to discover how the emphasis placed by feminist and queer theorists upon gender must always be considered within the context of the material conditions in which individuals articulate the possibilities of their lives.

We can now return to Foucault's critique of sexuality by recognizing its emphasis on the effort it requires of us to engage the categories of sexuality and gender. It is labor, and it is the labor of biopolitics, about which Foucault had much to say. Foucault's concept of biopolitics understands that how we define ourselves as sexual human beings tells us much about the intersection of our embodied, material selves and our ability to flourish—or not—economically and politically. It is not the case for Foucault that sexuality is part of the "merely" biological aspect of human life, whereas labor is more explicitly political. They go hand in hand. The world which Ennis del Mar and Jack Twist inhabit of the mid-twentieth-century western United States is one in which few opportunities arise for men with little education or experience of the world and this is expressed through the sexual relations in the film. The film's opening sequence depicts them applying for jobs at Joe Aguirre's office—a trailer in a bleak parking lot, where Ennis waits with nothing else to do and Jack arrives in a wheezing truck that is well past its prime. The jobs they sign on to do—watching sheep on a high mountain pasture in order to prevent attacks from coyotes—place them at virtually the lowest level of economic prosperity, in a world defined by ranching, mineral extraction, and the barest of local businesses that support such activities.

Ennis' biography, we later learn, includes the early death of his parents, an adolescence in his sister's household with spare attention given to him, a year of high school and the loss of his parents' ranching business, the net effect placing him on one of the lowest ladders of the social world. Jack's story, told more sparingly and only becoming available to the spectator in glimmers, seems parallel to Ennis'. Indeed, the fact that the two are not offered as cowboys—despite their boots and Stetson hats—but are specifically sheepherders, places them a rung below men who might at the very least be able to inhabit the myth of the independence and self-reliance of cowboys. Ennis and Jack might more closely be associated with shepherd dogs than with human society, and often the film's mise-en-scène affiliates them with the world of animals, natural forces, and predators than with human society, from which they find themselves at a great distance.

It is worth pausing to understand that *Brokeback Mountain*'s sense of the historical moment in which it is set counters the strong nostalgia of life for the period. Indeed, the summer in which its narrative begins—1963—figures often in the larger culture as a twilight of American greatness in the moment just prior to the assassination of President John Fitzgerald Kennedy and the unfolding of the so-called turbulent 1960s. It is a question whether such a vaunted sense of the moment is warranted (the 1950s were no less defined by social conflict, unease, and anomie), but Lee's film works against establishing a vision of the utopian America which is so often attached to the historical moment.

This insight matters to our discovery that, in order to make sense of *Brokeback Mountain*'s fictional world, we benefit from recognizing that the time in which Ennis, Jack, Alma, and Lureen live is far from utopian. The sole opportunity for prosperity appears in the form of Jack's father-in-law's business, which sells farm equipment in rural Texas, but aside from that the western United States of *Brokeback Mountain* is one of bleak farmsteads, a life above a laundromat and low-paying menial labor.

As a setting for understanding how the biopolitical power of that world is exerted upon the men and women in the film, we learn that the bond that emerges between the two men takes shape distinctly against the expectation (which both characters express) that they will marry and have children. The forms of compulsory masculinity available to these men link closely to the compulsory heterosexuality in which their gender and sexuality might unfold, and their ability to inhabit the masculine languages, behaviors, and appearances in which they have been raised assumes that this masculine deportment leads directly toward marriage and reproduction. This aspect is well worth emphasizing because the queer desires and practices they engage in have little meaning within the insistent assumption that they only are to be husbands and fathers.

If we follow this logic through the film's narrative, we can begin to see how the fact of their affection and desire for each other has a direct impact on their ability to function as economic actors—to work, in short—over the duration of their relationship. Several times, for example, we see them in dispute with their wives over the effect that their trips to the wilderness have upon the household and the fact that both Alma and Lureen are shown working to support their families as their husbands maintain low-paying jobs as ranch worker, rodeo rider, and tractor salesman to supplement their wives' labor to sustain their households.

Lastly, the figures of Alma and Lureen are themselves part of the biopolitics of *Brokeback Mountain's* historical era as much as they figure within the lives of the more central male characters because the women too are defined by the manner in which their economic status, their sexuality, and their sexual reproductive status are all co-constituted. In the sequence in which we see Alma and Ennis in sexual embrace in their bedroom and she asks that they use protection—that is a condom—Alma tells Ennis that she does not want more children beyond the two daughters they already are raising unless he can support them; he recoils from her and signals the beginning of his withdrawal from the marriage not because his ability to perform sexually within their marriage is frustrated—despite the implication discussed elsewhere that he has developed a preference for rear sexual penetration in intercourse and/or anal intercourse—but because his ideal of himself as a wage earner for their family has been impugned.

The film's raw depictions of the harshness of life in the western landscape tell us much about the fact of their deprivation not only from wealth, prosperity, and economic exchange but also from language and history itself. Recalling Ennis and Jack's confessional conversation discussed earlier, we discover that biopolitics here is about the denial of even language to those most in need of it. The deprivation and subsequent emergence of a shared language between the two men is the ground on which the sexual relations between the two will develop for each of them, and Foucault's admonition that it is in silences and what might develop out of such silences that the film's fantasy of their mutuality comes to life.

Part of the appeal of the film is its sense of historical possibility of a new life fashioned in this society of two, and it is worth noting how often the film seems to withhold dialogue in order to underscore the remarkable lack of a preexisting discourse for what the two men are experiencing. In this regard, *Brokeback Mountain* shapes a kind of utopia that is historically prior to the contemporary ways in which we think about sexuality and gender. Indeed, when the story begins to unfold in 1963 the viewer knows of the historical conditions in which sexual politics will change in the following decades in ways, of course, that the characters cannot. Only a few years later will the Stonewall riots of 1969, rightly or wrongly often located as a pivotal moment for the emergence of gay and lesbian political history, inaugurate the struggles of LGBQT activist movements.

If we seek an understanding of the film through the concepts that Foucault delineates, we should then begin with two crucial and parallel ideas: first, the film is not a factual representation of anything we know about homoerotic life among men in the historical period in which it is set, but a fantasy about such, and second, its appeal to us might derive from the fact that it does not traffic in any of the terms that we currently inhabit. It is no small irony that the film was often referred to in shorthand fashion as "the gay cowboy movie" because neither are Ennis or Jack cowboys—they are menial labor in the agricultural economy—nor are they gay. That term would have been incomprehensible to the world they inhabited and the sole reference made to any discernible identity politics which we might know about is when, after their first sexual encounter, Ennis tells Jack "I ain't no queer," to which Jack responds "I ain't either."

Here, we discover that the only form of language to which they might resort to describing their bond—"queer"—was solely pejorative and to be rejected by them as unable to name or describe what they are living through. The act of negation—of recognizing what name it is that they do *not* want to attached to them—forms the kind of situation Foucault has in mind in arguing that such names are regulatory. If we recall Foucault's insistence that confession emerged as a central technique for the repressive hypothesis' ability to enjoin individuals to employ regulatory sexual discourses to produce a sexuality for themselves, the remarkable silence within *Brokeback Mountain* about the naming of identities—("gay," "queer," and the like) or sexual practices (which are visually implied but never discussed by the characters) forms part of the appeal of the film because it allows spectators to contemplate an historical era in which such discourses about sexuality were not available even as sexual practices and related forms of intimacy develop between the film's two central characters. Further, the film's withholding of such typical language about sexuality and gender forms its inadvertently utopian dimensions around the topic.

By this, I mean that *Brokeback Mountain* does not solely depict a fantasized world of intimate and sexual possibilities between its characters by claiming to be about a particular place and era that seems prior to the ideas about sexuality and gender which our discourses shape for us (it does indeed do that), but the film also asserts the possibility of living without such regulatory practices as, in fact, highly possible and indeed quite possibly appealing. If Foucault's theories help to explain and to historicize sexuality in the modern era, the global appeal of Lee's film comes from its capacity that such forms of seemingly discourseless sexuality are another possibility for us. Thus, while the particular outcome of the narrative itself is quite dismal—Jack and Ennis do have the opportunity to share the intimate daily life which Jack, at least, yearns for—the film is utopian because it speculates upon a different set of undisclosed meanings for sex that our confessional compulsions do not begin to consider as even possible.

To make sense of these distinctions, let us consider how the men in *Brokeback Mountain* would have their sex, gender, and sexuality explained through the categories of gender and sexuality. Ennis del Mar and Jack Twist are biological cis-males—or, at least, we assume this to be valid and the narrative offers no information to contradict this idea. They are gendered as white, working-class masculine men within the expectations of mid-twentieth-century rural western United States: their clothing, manner of speech, forms of labor, and ideas about marriage and reproduction seem to coincide with our understanding of masculinity in that particular historical setting.

Their sexuality, though, would be the sexological surprise that emerges within the film's narrative because these men's masculinity typically suggests the sexual aim toward women (whose own relations of sex to gender we could limn in similar fashion). The pressure that *Brokeback Mountain*—indeed, its scandalous status—places upon its viewers derives from the sexological explanation that most spectators have inherited—not least, in the compulsory heterosexual ideals of contemporary societies—and which confounds the relation between masculinity and same-sex desire and same-sex practice.

Within the mythologies of gender and performativity, perhaps no other figure within contemporary culture sustains ideas about the attributes of masculinity than the cowboy: strength and an indifference to pain, the capacity for solitude and the avoidance of social interaction, the formation of identity through labor, forthrightness to the point of bluntness, and a need to find connection with the natural world of the western landscape. That these are a set of traits associated with one particular form of idealized masculine performance is worth keeping in mind because other masculinities are appropriate to other social roles, such as we might find in the masculinities performed in other cultural and cinematic genres, not least in the romantic comedy or the musical. The emblem of the cowboy, though, enjoys a unique status as an ideal of masculinity that endures, even as the genre of the Western itself might wane in popularity over time.

How, though, is such masculinity *performed*? And how might we discover this within the film? The acting of Heath Ledger and Jake Gyllenhaal offers important clues in terms of how each fulfills particular expectations of sanctioned masculinity while simultaneously seeking, as performance so often does, to conceal itself *as performance*: to seem entirely natural and without effort. That we as spectators are encouraged not to understand this dimension of performance places demands on us to critically frame it and to disentangle the effects that such enactment create.

We discover the film's performative masculinities through a number of critical avenues related to the racial, classed, regional, and erotic traits which are imbedded within Ledger's and Gyllenhaal's acting within the film. First, we should note that the film emphasizes their whiteness and plays on assumptions about the American west (and the Western genre) as a place of white social life. This makes a certain sense if we frame the history of European and white American colonization as the context in which the story plays out, and particular features of their characters which Ledger and Gyllenhaal's performances emphasize help to reaffirm an idea of that white colonization as one of the working classes.

Ledger's acting—which earned him an Academy Award nomination and which was the more widely acclaimed within popular and critical commentary on the film—underscores his character as taciturn, socially awkward, and at odds to make social connection with others, be they his wife, daughters, employers, or his closest friend and lover. Ennis del Mar, as Ledger interprets him, maintains a hunched posture, seems challenged to maintain eye contact, and speaks in a manner that makes apparent just how difficult it is for him even to get his words out.

We can perceive, though, how the figure of Ledger's version of Ennis serves as an emblem of more than simply character biography or a conduit for narrative information, and the popular critical responses to the film reveal the attitudes and expectations that such a performance confirms or defies for its audiences. In their analysis of the film's reception, Brenda Cooper and Edward C. Pease have argued that the film's reception by many reviewers revealed distinct and contradictory ideas about what the film meant to its critics, and these frames, as Cooper and Pease call them, take three forms: the universal, the peculiar, and the past homophobic.

As they argue, "Whether we see the film as 'universal' or 'peculiar,' is a paradoxical invisibility for queer identity, and yields a third frame in which homophobia is represented as a relic of the past."[1] Cooper and Pease's analysis of 113 popular reviews of the film up to 2008 suggests that critics were generally in agreement in their positive endorsement of the film, but that the terms in which they sought to approve of its message were in fact inconsistent and reveal discordant assumptions about how to interpret the film and, by implication, its performative dimensions. One form of review embraced the idea of its apparent universality because the possibility of emotional and sexual intimacy between men in the historical moment of the film's setting was said to reveal that possibility for seemingly any historical moment and that, thus, *Brokeback Mountain* is, as Cooper and Pease paraphrase the reviews, "a romance like any other." One important aspect of this response, they note, is that such commentary sought to partition the film from having any explicit political agenda, a significant claim in light of the film's appearance during debates in the United States and elsewhere about the rights of LGBQT people to marry, to serve in the military, and to enjoy regulatory protections from harassment and violence. This idea, Cooper and Pease argue, resulted in the problem that "whatever the critics may have hoped or intended, the universal framing strategies work to 'un-queer' Ennis and Jack, in effect positioning them within the safe boundaries of familiar heterosexual cinema."[2]

Distinct from the universalizing critical responses, Cooper and Pease discern interpretations of the film that focus upon the film's particular rendering of white masculinity in the tradition of the Hollywood Western. Here, Ledger and Gyllenhaal's acting is said to be no different from the performances in Westerns by actors such as Gary Cooper, John Wayne, and Clint Eastwood, performances that embrace the reticent, physically robust, and emotionally withdrawn masculinity associated with these male film stars. A typical review asserted that Ennis and Jack are not "stereotypical gay men," but "rugged outdoorsmen and individualists who'd be at home in any John Wayne movie."[3] While the impulse here, Cooper and Pease suggest, might have been to frame the film's depictions of masculinity as part of a longer history of performance in the Western and to seem to normalize them, "the overall discourse of these reviews works to keep the two men in the closet." They conclude that the "peculiar" critical reading of *Brokeback Mountain* as simply a new installment in Western gender performance resists understanding a link between the film's moment of production and larger political debates about queer sexuality: "Whatever the reviewers' open-minded intentions, their framing strategies nonetheless are mired within a heterosexist language that does not—or cannot—accommodate queers and their subjectivities."[4]

The connection that Cooper and Pease see such reviews as unwilling to make is that between the homophobic strains of the current public and political sphere at the moment of the film's release and the fact of a homophobic past that is not identical with it. In other words, by embracing the masculine ideals of the Western's male performance in prior moments, such critics sidestep the fact of having to make sense of the film not solely as a comment on the world of 1960s and 1970s Wyoming and Texas but as well of the current milieu of marriage equality, the end of don't-ask-don't-tell policies, and LGBQT politics.

This allows for the third critical frame to emerge, according to Cooper and Pease, within the trope of a homophobia that apparently no longer is relevant to the present era. Most critics, they assert, "frame homophobia and queer discrimination as a relic of the bad old days that American society has left behind since *Brokeback*'s 1963 timeframe," and that "reviewers were twice as likely to frame issues of prejudice and violence against gays as a past problem than they were to connect the film to continuing contemporary threats confronting sexual minorities." The net effect of the three frames that Cooper and Pease identify is that the film is neutralized as a commentary upon present-day ongoing discrimination and violence against queer people, because reviewers insisted upon reading the film as about how heterosexual men might have sexual and emotional intimacy. And, to a degree, given that the categories of sexual identity which have emerged in the years since those of the film's fictional world were unavailable to the men within the film, Ennis and Jack had little possibility of "coming out." Within the critical frame of performance theory, though, we should ask how its versions of male gendering enabled the critical frames that Cooper and Pease identify within reviews of the film.

A vitalizing contrast can help to see the limits that Cooper and Pease identify and another way to understand the implications of this form of conjunctural analysis within queer theory would be to see it played out in a very different setting, such as we find in the effect of *Brokeback Mountain* among audiences in the People's Republic of China. The film garnered significant attention among Chinese viewers, despite the fact that the Chinese government was squeamish about the film's depictions of male same-sex sexuality and did not permit release of the film into public exhibition spaces. Chinese viewers were undeterred and the film was distributed without legal permissions in gray-market distribution channels and figured within queer Chinese discourse as an expression of the constraints on queer men and women in, on the one hand, a repressive political regime and, on the other, the conservatism of long-standing Confucian values that emphasize the needs of shared life of family and community above the need of the individual for expression or pleasure.

Chris Berry describes this tension in terms of how Lee's films that are most vividly associated with Chinese culture, history, and politics are organized by the genre of the "family ethics film," which he describes as similar but not identical to the Hollywood melodrama. In Hollywood film, "The film usually ends with the formation of a couple." On the other hand, in the Chinese family-ethics film, "The struggle is between an individual's sense of duty and their selfish personal desires. Duty tends to triumph."[5]

Berry's discussion of the film situates its Chinese queer viewers within the counterposing forces of compliance with familial priority and the invention and development of relations that do not conform to the traditional family configuration, and the appeal of *Brokeback Mountain* for its Chinese audience resided in the film's apparent refusal finally to endorse either position. The film's conclusion leaves unresolved the possible outcome of Ennis and Jack having formed a more enduring, even domestic, relation because Jack's death forestalls for Ennis having to make a decision to do so.

Significant for Berry's reading of the film within the context of its Chinese reception is the fact that not solely were queer Chinese men and women—"gays" and "lalas" in the local usage—engaged in the film around this ambiguity, but many Chinese straight-identified women did as well. This, as Berry suggests, is part of a pattern of same-sex male romances finding receptive viewers among straight women and this "visible culture of gay male love stories for female consumption has developed in East Asia."[6]

William F. Schroeder links this phenomenon to the interest in China to have a director of Chinese ethnic heritage (Lee was born and raised in Taiwan before immigrating to the United States) identified as a maker of globalized film that extends the terms of Chinese culture to other audiences; as Schroeder writes, "Many queer Chinese people understand that if a famous straight director with Chinese roots could release this film to worldwide acclaim and then be nominated for and win a host of prestigious awards, being queer and Chinese could then finally be legitimated in everyone's eyes, including those of the people at home."

If we draw together the several features of *Brokeback Mountain*'s reception in the PRC which Berry and Schroeder describe, we discover that the film's racial and gender politics allegorize a set of concerns different from those we might find in audiences in North America or Europe. (And, we should be at pains to remember that viewers in those latter spaces are not monolithic in their thoughts about the film.) The way that the film crystallizes for its Chinese viewers an intensely felt bind between one form of social demand via the family to support its ethical ideals and a modern, "western" ethos of self-expression via gender and sexuality; the possibility of reading its same-sex romance as an allegory for what Chinese straight women see as homologous with their own position between family and individualism; and the pleasure for Chinese audiences to see how its director is interpreting these problems within a sensibility shaped by his Chinese heritage all point us toward seeing how the gender and racial dimensions of the film can mean very different things depending upon the context of where a film appears. In the terms of performance theory, the text maintains a power—it has an effect—often in ways that cannot be anticipated not only by its makers but also by viewers and critics in different places and contexts.

The Chinese response to the film is what Eve Sedgwick means by a reparative reading. The paranoid reading—the hermeneutics of suspicion—would constitute the bulk of the present book, emphasizing as it does the acts of violence toward the two central figures which always lurk just outside the film frame seeming to wait to interject into the fragments of joy which Jack and Ennis can make for themselves. A reparative reading would ask how, according to Sedgwick, "related practices of reparative knowing may lie, barely recognized and little explored, at the heart of many histories of gay, lesbian and queer intertextuality."[7] By intertextuality, we can understand her to sense that there always reside unanticipated connections between different texts (such as films) and the larger world in which they circulate, and as much we must exert ourselves to discover, in the terms of paranoid reading, the anti-queer world that shapes them, we must also beware that this pursuit limits our sense of how these texts circulate in unexpected ways to the very people—often queer, sometimes not—who vitally need them.

Berry and Schroeder's research guides us toward the queer Chinese reception of Lee's film and is one such intertextual and queer reparative instance about which Sedgwick's writing provides us the theoretical language to understand. No one would argue that any of *Brokeback Mountain*'s makers—from Proulx, to Lee, McMurtry, or Gyllenhaal—had in mind such an outcome, and yet queer men and women in the PRC found the film a vehicle for thinking about the challenges which being queer present to their lives. Schroeder puts it best when he asserts about the queer Chinese response to *Brokeback Mountain*, "that dismissing *tongzhi*[8] interests in romanticism—which may be another way to describe affectivity—as misinformed or politically wrongheaded violates the hopefulness of their liberatory endeavor to understand predicaments beyond the limitations of place and time."[9]

Gender performance and the film Western

Turning now to the insights that queer performance theory can offer to us about the film, we focus upon the genre in which the film is situated. Most popular films align themselves with a recognizable genre, some of which wane in popularity over time while others arise in new and freshly defined terms. The various genres with which most contemporary viewers are familiar—the romantic comedy, the action-adventure, the superhero film—accompany genres that have enjoyed greater popularity in prior historical moments: the historical epic, the film noir, and the musical.

Brokeback Mountain's generic identity is most centrally that of the Western, a type of film that appeared early in the classical Hollywood studio film at the beginning of the twentieth century and that enjoyed a large viewership through the mid-twentieth century. While Westerns continue to be produced, the form occupies a curious status in the contemporary practices of the dominant US corporate film mode, and this can tell us much about the particular status of the Western as a cultural anchor for the importance of ideologies of American national identity, for changing notions of gender (most notably in terms of sanctified ideas about masculinity), and for ideas about individualism within the constraints of community.

Critics and historians of the Western generally agree that the genre includes several key formal, ideological, and aesthetic hallmarks that distinguish it from other genres: the mise-en-scène includes images of the American west as it is idealized as a vast landscape, often cinematically framed for admiration of the natural beauty of the western United States' mountains and deserts, while the human figures within the frame are typified as adventuresome men (and, sometimes but rarely, women) who seek to forge new lives for themselves in an ostensibly limitless and apparently unpopulated world. Worth noting about the genre is that the historical western United States depicted within the Western genre was, in point of fact, inhabited by Native Americans and procured by European settlement mostly through violence and colonization, and this is one of the abiding problems for the Western film, but this fact is obscured by the psychology of the colonizing men and women around whom the Western film organizes its concerns.

More particular features of the mise-en-scène typically emerge around the central figure of the Western, the cowboy, and the presence of the cowboy in the Western is both aesthetic and of urgent concern both ideologically and narratively. The cowboy allows the Western to articulate its persistent concern with the problem of the individual being unable either to conform to the social norms that constrain his freedom or to endure the solitude and exclusion which the landscape paradoxically makes possible and simultaneously enforces. This has shaped the cowboy into a figure of now mythic status as the man—and it is almost always a man—who neither finds a meaningful identity within social life nor in his lonely status as a man who seeks a relation with the larger natural world. Thus, what we witness repeatedly over the many cinematic versions of the Western appearing in the past century is the story of a man who is trapped between civilization and nature, and feminist critics have noticed that there is a conjoined figure of the woman who serves as an intermediary to bring both into alignment.

The woman in the Western, though, troubles the conflict rather than resolves it because she can never, within the idealized versions of masculinity which the Western endorses, be the equal of the cowboy. While in many Westerns at the film's conclusion the cowboy resolves himself to "settling" with a women in heterosexual marriage, the resolution seems an unsatisfying solution to the problem that gives the Western its status. (Notable exceptions ratify this sense of an only partial conclusion, such as in John Ford's 1956 film *The Searchers*, where the heroic cowboy reconsolidates the white family and then summarily exits from it in the film's final frame.)

The version of idealized masculinity that the Western insists upon is one where physical violence is the sole solution to most challenges presented within social life and the central thematic and narrative emphasis within Westerns appears in the fight: fist fights, gun fights, bar brawls, turf wars, Indian-killing, the list goes on. Such conflicts are often ostensibly justified within the Western as a means to protect others who are more vulnerable—women and children—but the Western is frequently less interested in the civilizing values associated with such apparently weaker figures than it is in the bloodshedding and violence which its aesthetic has developed over the past century of cinema.

The performance of masculinity-as-violence within the Western and its particular associated aesthetics have waned in past half-century as other genres have taken over the project of reaffirming masculine violence, action-adventure, superhero, and suspense films most notably. But, the ideological project of sanctifying physical violence and brutality within the Westerns remains a central myth within contemporary popular culture to such an extent that *Brokeback Mountain* can take advantage of that myth in order to explore how such masculinity might conjoin with same-sex sexuality.

The linkage of violence and sexuality is not so difficult a thing as one might initially imagine about the Western, and an often repeated scene within Westerns depicts challenges between men to various contests—not least, the shoot-out—and lends itself to our reading such scenes as moments of tacit seduction. Further, the Western, despite its proclamations of virility, is not hostile to homoerotic bonding as such, as often Westerns have subtly managed to imply, but never confirm, physical attraction and intimacy between men in the Western narrative. If women have diminished or often nonexisting roles within the Western, the genre has been about men and, in the cinematic dimension, physically beautiful men. Some of the most handsome male actors in the Hollywood studio system were associated with the genre, Henry Fonda, Gary Cooper, Errol Flynn, Montgomery Clift, to name a few.

The Western secures its appeal to viewers because it never fully resolves or discloses the tension between being a lone male and being a male in the company of men with whom the most idealized of social bonds are played out—but played out through physical conflict and violence. The Western's emphasis on the existential drama of a man defending himself against the elements and against hostile others cannot avoid but raise the question of how such like-minded masculine men with shared ideas about the world might spend time in each other's company. As a partial and tacit solution to this existential dilemma, the Western has often offered the possibility of a homosocial and, possibly, homoerotic alliance between men which gives relief to the problem of the single man who cannot abide by the limits of "civilized" life. Indeed, as early as 1948, in an article that suggested that much of the canon of American literature contained within it an underlying simultaneous unease and desire for homoerotic affiliation, Leslie Fiedler in "Come Back to the Raft Ag'in, Huck Honey,"[10] suggested that part of the appeal of the Western adventure story was its ability to fantasize about forms of male same-sex social contact— here, in Mark Twain's *Huck Finn*—which the racist and hypermasculine imagination had rendered off-limits. Fielder's account is hardly affirming of male same-sex sexuality, but its appearance in its particular historical moment indicates that the Western had long carried within it the implication of male same-sex erotics.

The film Western's ability to depict such possible affiliations between men was shaped by the fact of the Hollywood Production Code's insistence that "perversion" (largely a euphemistic code word for homosexuality) was excluded from the corporate studio product and thus most Westerns could only allude to such possibilities. Further, we should note that it was probably not the intent of most directors and writers within Hollywood to depict such forms of sexuality, although in a few instances the sexual play implied between cowboys is nearly impossible to ignore, such as a scene within *Red River* (Howard Hawks, 1948) in which Cherry Valance (John Ireland) and Matt Garth (Montgomery Clift) converse about their mutual admiration for each other's pistols. "You know," Cherry says, handling Matt's gun, "There are only two things more beautiful than a good gun: a Swiss watch or a woman from anywhere. You ever had a Swiss watch?" The implication here is that Cherry suspects that Matt is more likely to have interest in a reliable timekeeper than in a woman.

This tacit relation between the Western and male homoerotic alliance frames the manner in which *Brokeback Mountain* was claimed to be the first explicit "gay cowboy" film, and the problem of understanding the complicated status of same-sex sexuality for the genre of the Western provides us the opportunity to see how queer readings of an ostensibly queer popular film relate to the history of previous installments of the genre because *Brokeback Mountain* poses the question of how depictions of queer sexuality reshape our interpretation of the historical past—both the past that gave rise to representations such as Hollywood films *and* the past imagined within such representations. In other words, like it or not, *Brokeback Mountain* queered the Western film genre.

This last point helps us to recall that the Western films produced within the period of the classical Hollywood film (defined as those US corporate films produced between 1917 and 1960) depicted an idea about a period in history that had already concluded, a period whose defining characteristics had been superseded by new forms of social, economic, and political life. The west—its landscape and ecology, its history, its social groups, and its ideologies—that the Western represents was hardly a world that audiences could have been expected to recognize or remember and yet the genre made powerful claims about the kinds of ideas that Americans were thought to expect from the popular cinema that they consumed. Not least among these ideas were those pertaining to gender and sexuality, and one of the defining characteristics about the Hollywood Western—*Brokeback Mountain* included—is that it can manufacture its versions of gendering and sexuality by asserting their having been a part of a past that shaped the present moment.

We can begin to understand how a film and its genre are historical in this regard when we examine the various elements contained within a genre and how they relate one to the other as a form of commentary on previous installments of the genre as a more recent production such as Lee's film comments upon them. In the context of the present discussion, we can begin to see how the features of the Western sustain a performance of gender that is not solely located in terms of the body, but is part of the larger historical fantasy about the past.

Thus, it might seem counterintuitive to think of a landscape as gendered, but worth recalling in the present context is that the landscape is an aspect of the mise-en-scène within a particular genre of the cultural production called Hollywood. If we were discussing another form of the mise-en-scène within a different genre—say, clothing styles in a film melodrama—this idea of how the depiction of the natural environment within *Brokeback Mountain*'s narrative contributes to its handling of questions of sexuality and gender performance emerges as the primary aspect of the film's visual field in which human freedom and possibility might develop.

It is important here to recall that the film Western has been, since its emergence at the start of the twentieth century, a cultural production in which the tension between individual human agency and the social demand for cooperation, indeed for obedience, can be played out. Further, this tension figures within the Western through the depiction of the openness of the vast American west, where far horizons and open skies suggest endless possibilities through the ideology of the frontier of colonial expansion by Europeans. This form of freedom offered by the ostensibly open land is fraught within the film Western because it makes possible an irreconcilable contradiction from which the genre draws its energies: the limitless exploration of the world by the individual away from the social group in a natural world that can easily destroy him. However, what is so appealing to the individual—his (and it is emphatically within the Western *his*) newfound possibility to explore the world—in fact appeals because of that menace contained within it. Thus, nature entices and threatens the individual who enters the wilderness without protection from the social group; the lone figure on the land is both free and vulnerable at the same time.

The landscape in the Western plays an important role in the genre, a role that becomes even more complicated within

Brokeback Mountain's depictions of gender and sexuality. In a prescient analysis of the role that the landscape plays in the Western, Jane Tompkins writes that "it is the genius of the Western that it seems to make the land speak for itself."[11] What the land seems to be saying, though, is often difficult to discern and contradictory because, as Tompkins continues, "in the end, the land is everything to the hero, it is both destination and way. He courts it, struggles with it, defies it, conquers it, and lies down with it at night."[12]

For Tompkins, the landscape within the Western mediates between the *idea* of an unsocial, unhuman world that surrounds the lone individual man within it and the *reality* of the social world he has left behind. The landscape materializes a relation that can be lived—can be eaten, breathed, physically felt—by the hero within the genre. It becomes, in short, a character within the narrative and one with whom the hero has an intimate, indeed an erotic bond. The hero, in Tompkins' account, falls in love with the landscape of the west despite knowing that its harshness and extremes might at any moment wound or kill him.

The world of human civilization offers no real alternative to this vexed bond between hero and land; while the world of human society—identified so often within the Western as "the town"—might seem to offer shelter and comfort, in truth the hero finds that he must leave the beloved (and threatening) natural world and all that it offers in order to retreat to the pleasures—and forms of weakness and characterlessness—to be found in town. Shared human life appeals to the hero, but for all the wrong reasons: it alienates the hero from himself and from the truths to be found in the brutal existential encounter with the forces of the natural environment. As Tompkins notes, "Town fills basic needs, but basic though they are, they are precisely the needs that have to be denied because of what their satisfaction inevitably entails. *Town seduces*. [Emphasis my own]."[13]

Brokeback Mountain's depiction of the western landscape does not stray far from the account that Tompkins offers her readers, but the discovery of the possibility of intimate romantic and sexual bonding between men within the genre offers a remarkable opportunity to see in more refined fashion the implications both of what the genre has understood about itself *and* to discover what happens when the tacit homoerotic valences of what has often existed, in subtle and unarticulated fashion within the genre over its longer historical duration, are made explicit to the viewer. That is, *Brokeback Mountain* narrates in innovative fashion a version of sexuality within the Western that has been historically prohibited to be explicitly articulated as such—but not solely within the terms which Tompkins describes. Human sexuality is typically disallowed for the hero in the Western because in its heterosexual dimension it is associated with femininity, the town, and with weakness. At the same time, homoerotic affiliation traditionally within the genre expresses itself through violent conflict while heterosexual sexuality—associated with the feminine—as Tompkins avers, "seduces the hero." By making the tacit same-sex pleasure of the Western explicit for the viewer, *Brokeback Mountain* reverses this expectation because the male heroes of the film discover a different kind of sexual intimacy within and associated with the natural world that fulfills them in a way that no other domestic or civilized human bond might.

Brokeback Mountain combines that intimate bond between the hero and the landscape and the hero and the (impossible) human social world into the figure of another human: another man. While other prior Westerns, most notably *Lonesome Cowboys* (Andy Warhol and Paul Morrissey, 1968) and *Midnight Cowboy* (John Schlesinger, 1969) drew their narrative and spectatorial energies from the erotic charge of the stereotypical cowboy, those films organized their depictions of their central masculine figures within the more usual constrained circumstances in which the hero himself was an object of erotic fascination for the spectator. The key difference for *Brokeback Mountain*'s depiction is its innovation in moving this combined figure—of landscape and human—into the foreground for its spectators. While other men and women within the narrative—most notably Joe Aguirre and Alma Del Mar—might speculate about the intimate sexual bond between Ennis and Jack, we the film's viewers are informed (in as explicit a fashion as the contemporary Hollywood product might allow) of how the film depicts the landscape of the Western as it signifies desire and fulfillment.

A key distinction which the film's mise-en-scène makes within its representation of the western landscape and which informs the manner in which the landscape has an erotic symbolic function is that between the mountains and the desert. As the film's title emphasizes, Brokeback Mountain is the heart of the film's sense of the utopian queer possibilities and many critics and viewers have noted how the film's visual ensemble of images draws the spectator's attention to the scale and impact of the mountainous landscape of the North American west. The film's saturated chromatic scale emphasizes the green lush ecology (Ennis and Jack are, after all, on the mountain in order to watch the sheep who graze on the mountain's verdant grasses) and the scope of the film frame repeatedly throughout the film, but especially in the first third of its running time, makes a point of the vastness of the mountains.

This scale is no accident for the film's performative aspects. *Brokeback Mountain*'s panoramic shots of the mountain in sunshine and in storm tell us about the dynamic and unpredictable possibilities which the natural world heralds for the film's central characters. If the mundane world of human social life below the mountain prohibits closeness and intimacy between men, or cannot even imagine it, the mountain makes possible all manner of new experiences for those who are able to enter its monumental sense of limitlessness. This explains why, once Jack and Ennis leave Brokeback Mountain, the bond that they sustain over the next two decades will continually see them returning to the mountain and have them make reference to it as a form of shorthand about the shared life they found there.

This sense of union to be found in the western mountain landscape is hardly new to the Western for, as Ed Buscombe writes, "From the earliest Westerns located in the Rockies of Colorado to the classics of the 1950s and 1960s, mountain scenery has been used to authenticate 'Westernness.'"[14] The authenticity of the Western, though, is not solely about its locale, but about the use of landscape to alert viewers to the concerns of the genre, which Andre Bazin suggests "encompass the aesthetic, sociological, moral, psychological, political and erotic."[15] Buscombe continues that the landscape "is an aesthetic object. Its function is to be gazed at, in an act of reverential contemplation" because, "nature is conceived as essentially unspoiled." He suggests about the Western that "mountain scenery in this tradition seems inescapably bound to a kind of spiritual uplift, as if the verticality of the mountains were in some way a metaphor of their effect upon the observer. In Hollywood cinema, and in the Western in particular, mountain scenery could be said to function as a substitute for religion, a way of introducing a secular spiritual dimension."[16]

Mountains within Westerns are where the most exalted human experiences emerge, and mountains alter the course of the narrative. Buscombe sees this as a form of secular spirituality, where contact with the divine or metaphysical or an experience approximate to it becomes possible in ways not seemingly elsewhere, and Ennis and Jack's movement up the mountain leads them to the symbolic space where transformations within the Western occur.

The film's very first image announces this idea in its establishing shot as our eye moves over a long distance from valleys in the near foreground toward the silhouette of the mountains in the distance; across this panorama moves the lights of the truck in which Ennis has hitchhiked a ride. His traversal—parallel to the mountains but not yet toward them—signals the preparatory question for the film: What will it take to transform these men? The answer, as Buscombe's history of the Western's iconography tells us, will be found in the vertical movement away from the town.

Only after the narrative establishes the situation for Jack and Ennis to ascend will the film's action begin to take place, and worth noting in the transition from town to nature-on-the-mountain is the presence of the very economic motive for all that unfolds: sheep. In a key shot that signals the two characters' travel into the mountain range, we discover masses of sheep accompanying them. The presence of animals in *Brokeback Mountain*'s queer Western draws our attention to the fact that the Western's idealized landscape has from its earliest versions in painting and photography typically been a highly domesticated notion of nature, where the traditions of depicting the landscape within Westerns follows in the practice of asserting that the landscape must be made meaningful for the viewer. The most significant meanings attributed to the west have been, as Buscombe notes, a "mixing [of] the pastoral and the romantic in equal parts."[17]

The inclusion of the livestock functions to signal a nature that includes the objects of human society and makes the mountain into a kind of pasture or garden to be cultivated. It is not too ambitious to think that this pastoral and romantic setting depict the Edenic scene where the two men begin their love relation. Indeed, in one brief shot included in the sequence in which they migrate to the mountain, we see Jack tenderly holding a lamb as he nurses its hoof, an image that activates a long tradition of divine and maternal love which seeks to transform.

The opening third of the film shapes the mountain landscape as, to reiterate Buscombe, "pastoral and romantic in equal parts," and while most of the critical commentary upon the film has been devoted to the sexual bond that emerges between Ennis del Mar and Jack Twist in light of this sequence, surprisingly little discussion has noted the nature of the emotional bond that develops between them and in which their sexual contact takes shape. That bond is largely romantic, and the narrative here conforms to some of the typical features of the romance: trust, intimacy, humor, teasing, vulnerability, openness, anger, tenderness all develop within this portion of the narrative. Jack and Ennis become a conjoined couple who sleep together, converse, cook, bathe, urinate and defecate, and argue, negotiate, and share a life, well before they clumsily find their way toward sexual awareness and contact.

This pairing becomes possible both practically because they are far from the social life of the town—which would in this period not condone such a practice—and also symbolically, because the mountain's function within the Western tells its viewers of new kinds of life that have not yet been realized. Thus, within the queer pastoral mountain landscape we witness a queer romantic relation.

This queering of the Western mountain pictorial tradition results in important consequences for the unfolding psychology of *Brokeback Mountain*'s characters, with three particular moments to which I would draw our attention. The first is in the moment in which Joe Aguirre, the shepherds' boss, discovers the sexual play between Jack and Ennis. This narrative information is given to the spectator when we witness a shot in which the two men wrestle and embrace with their shirts off; the film offers this image initially through an unattributed long-range shot that is slightly distorted. The blurred image turns out to be the point-of-view vision beheld by Aguirre as he gazes through his binoculars and it is the first confirmation we have of someone besides the two men knowing of their relation.

Interestingly, Aguirre does not immediately act upon this information, although he coolly rides into the high mountain camp and informs Jack of his uncle's illness, this being the apparent reason for Aguirre's journey. Later, the two men will learn that their season on Brokeback Mountain has ostensibly been curtailed because of inclement weather, and whether or not this is an alibi for Aguirre to effectively terminate the men's employment remains ambiguous. Much later, Jack will learn that Aguirre suspects the sexual dimension of his and Ennis' relation when he returns several years after the summer of 1963 to seek employment and Aguirre caustically informs him that "you guys wasn't getting paid to leave the dogs to babysit the sheep while you stemmed the rose."

In order to make sense of Aguirre's discovery of Jack and Ennis' having "stemmed the rose" within the queer pastoral of *Brokeback Mountain*, we should recall that his initial discovery is made while beholding the scene through binoculars. The framing technique here underscores the sense that Aguirre cannot understand the scene unfolding before him because he looks *at* the mountainous terrain but does not dwell *within* it. Nature's impact upon him is nil, and thus he cannot, within the terms of Tompkins or Buscombe, ever be the genuine Western hero. Spending his time in a trailer in town with his feet up on his desk, he is immune to the transformative effects of the natural environment and thus beholds that environment as a thing outside himself rather than an engulfing place that alters human experience. Indeed, his scorn for the two men derives perhaps as much from their ecstatic experience on the mountain as much as it does from their "perverse" sexuality.

There is a paradox at hand, though, because if Aguirre cannot comprehend the nature of what is unfolding before him because of the mediating and distancing effects of lensing technology, how is the spectator of *Brokeback Mountain*—and, more generally, the Western film—any different? We, like Aguirre, witness the story through a technology (cinema) that distances us from the action; we cannot benefit from the utopian possibilities of the Western landscape in the ways that those who live within it might. Here, we should recall the guiding ideology of the Western film which suggests that the natural landscape of the American west is so powerful that even its very image can transform. Buscombe reminds us that some of the earliest Westerns were filmed in the eastern United States—most notably, *The Great Train Robbery* (1903), which was filmed in New Jersey—but that one of the most important aspects of the Western has been the need for primary photography on site in the western landscape and that, as soon as the US corporate film industry had migrated west early in its history, it quickly began to shoot on location in the American mountains and deserts. Buscombe links this emphasis on producing the images of the west for the Western to the romanticist movement, which considered nature in its powerful and sublime dimensions as producing positive and important changes in the person who beholds it, even if that occurs through paintings, photographs, and films. Thus, if the spectator cannot enjoy the benefits of dwelling within the natural environment which the Western depicts, they can receive such benefits through the telegraphed cinematic image of that environment.

A second moment that is conjoined with that above and which is worth emphasizing for our understanding of *Brokeback Mountain*'s queer pastoral performativity occurs in Jack and Ennis' return to Brokeback Mountain, and this return is most powerfully signaled by a shot that has become emblematic of the film. When, after their initial passionate reunion in town—where they kiss on the stairs below Ennis and Alma's apartment and then smoke in each other's arms while lying in a motel room—we see them later in the mountains as they strip their clothing and leap from a butte above a river into the water below. Their leap returns them to the lush and green fecundity of the mountains and this reentry quite explicitly hearkens to images taken from nineteenth-century American visual culture: the male nude in the natural setting. (One of the most important source images for this moment in the film is Thomas Eakins' 1884 painting, *The Swimming Hole*, whose depiction of nude white men diving and swimming in a verdant riverscape offers an idealized notion of male beauty within a bucolic world.)

Here, Jack and Ennis' migration back to the mountain contrasts sharply with the sequence appearing before it, where Alma's startled and hurt discovery of their kiss and embrace on the stairs brings only heartache and confusion. Unlike us, Alma cannot see the men in the Western's mountainous scenery, scenery whose vastness abruptly coincides with the cramped and cluttered interior life of the shabby apartment she shares with Ennis and their daughters. The film here suggests that Alma, especially because she is a woman, cannot know what the western natural environment of the Western makes possible, and in this light we should recall that the Western's preoccupation with masculinity—and especially white, working-class, rural masculinity—is hardly exceeded or critiqued within this film.

Furthermore, the combination of the two moments of discovery of Ennis and Jack's sexual affection for one another—Aguirre's through his binoculars, Alma's in the setting of the town—firmly reestablishes the Western's idea that the mountain is a sublime and transformative environment. This transformation cannot be seen or heard about, though; it must within the ideology of the Western be experienced and lived.

The third sequence that drives home the importance of the pastoral's effects on the characters appears on the morning in which Jack and Ennis leave their employment after the first summer on the high pastures. We witness Jack as he uses a rope to playfully lasso Ennis' ankles and then bring him to the ground; they subsequently wrestle in a way that recalls the scene in which Aguirre's suspicions are aroused about them. This moment of horseplay, however, quickly turns to aggression, as they physically brawl and each draws blood from the other. Here, the ugliest dimensions of "rugged" masculinity become apparent within Ledger and Gyllenhaal's performances.

This disharmony, the film's visual track tells us, results from the character's movement out of the natural environment of the mountain and back toward the social world of men and women which they had left behind. Their reentry into the community life of humans results in their physical abuse of each other and the fact of what has been affectionate horseplay while on the mountain now results in assault and violence; within the symbolic rules of the Western, in this sequence we learn again of *Brokeback Mountain*'s reverence for the "secular spiritual dimension" (to reiterate Buscombe) of the Western landscape.

After they have returned to the town of Signal, where they first met, they haltingly exchange good-byes, and we see Jack drive away in his derelict pickup while Ennis walks by the side of the road. In a point-of-view shot attributed to Jack, Ennis' figure is framed in the rearview mirror of the truck with the distant mountains' profile rising up behind him. Jack gazes—wistfully? longingly?—at Ennis before departing; Ennis, we subsequently discover, darts into an alley in order to crouch, vomit, and weep. A passing male figure glances at him, to which Ennis angrily growls, "What the fuck are you looking at?"

Each man responds in his own way to the experience of leaving the mountains and reentering the larger social world of the town, and the sequence elliptically foretells the effects that the summer on Brokeback Mountain has had upon them. In what will now become the motif of the story, Jack looks longingly upon Ennis while Ennis is reduced to the most basic of emotional utterances from the body: vomiting, tears and angry, hostile words.

If mountains sustain and nurture the men who enter them, then, deserts separate and alienate those same figures within the mise-en-scène of *Brokeback Mountain*. This idea about the desert as a scene of trial derives from long-standing practices within the genre regarding the use of the desert to signify any number of challenges—thirst, exhaustion, pursuit by Native Americans—to the heroic figures who cross but seldom inhabit the dry arid landscape. In an interesting turn of nomenclature and geography, in *Brokeback Mountain*'s fictive universe, "Texas" is the name given to the desert which forms the strong contrast to Wyoming's green Rocky Mountains.

Texas in *Brokeback Mountain* stands for a corrupted and domesticated form of the Western, and it is in the scenes set in Texas that we see Jack's easygoing masculinity neutered by his wife and his father-in-law. Having witnessed Jack's earlier attempts to pick up men in honky-tonk bars in the small towns where he rides in the rodeo, his first encounter with his future wife Lureen depicts her approaching him and initiating their subsequent sexual encounter in the back seat of her flashy convertible. Jack and Lureen's marriage requires him to move to Texas, where her father owns a prosperous tractor dealership and where Jack becomes a flunky to the business. As Lureen is seen, over the course of time, taking over the business from her father, she assumes her father's role of discounting Jack's talents and his role as a father and husband.

The important exception to this sense of the desert which Texas symbolizes within the film is over a Thanksgiving meal where Jack and his father engage in a domesticated form of the Western's shoot-out. As the family gathers around the table and Lureen instructs her son to turn the televised football game off, her father insists that the television remain on because football forms a crucial element in his grandson's well-being. Jack, however, insists that Lureen's wishes be honored and argues with his father-in-law, insisting that they are all gathered in his home and that his household rules be honored.

Here, we gain a sympathetic glimpse of Lureen as she suppresses a smile at the prospect of her self-important and boorish father having been, for once, socially demoted, and it is tempting to see Lureen and Jack as having a household and marriage which honors each of them. I would argue that the scene is one of pathos, though, because the victory for Jack is paltry and ultimately confirms the emptiness and materiality of the life he has found in Texas, which contrasts so remarkably with the life he yearns for in Wyoming with Ennis. Indeed, the gaudy and consumerist household in which he lives only confirms how soul-deadening—how much a desert—life in Texas is for him.

Jack's actual death in Texas opens the film's final chapter; if he has found little possibility for queer life in his aspirations for a shared life with Ennis in Wyoming, he is finally annihilated in Texas under circumstances which the film allows to remain ambiguous. Ennis learns of the event on a returned postcard that is part of the ritual through which we have seen them schedule time together over the years. He subsequently phones Lureen in order to gather the details about what has happened and their exchange does little to offer insight or comfort. Lureen, whom he has never met in person, offers a narrative in which Jack is reported to have died by himself having tried to fix a truck and having bled to death by the side of the road.

The sequence cuts between Ennis, who stands in a phone booth, and Lureen in her living room in Texas, and interposed with shots of them speaking, the sequence includes images of Jack and a group of men as he is attacked and beaten. These images are implied to be Ennis' fantastic expansion upon Lureen's version of things; they are fantasized by Ennis as the truer set of events by which Jack was most probably to die.

The ambiguity here implicates the audience in a significant problem for interpreting the film because whether or not we decide upon how valid Ennis' fantasy of Jack's death might be, the fact that he sees the conjunction between queer life and violent death offers insight into the stakes for Ennis of his association with Jack over the years. We should recall that Jack never tells Ennis of Joe Aguirre's derisive comment about them "stemming the rose" on Brokeback Mountain, so Ennis' idea about the violence that he sees Jack as victim to is the product of his much earlier association from childhood about the death of the local rancher whose body he was compelled by his father to bear witness to. Ennis has little reason to think that Jack's knowledge about others knowing of their bond is not grounded within that reality.

Ennis' troubled sense of Jack's death is hardly warranted by any narrative information we might have about the circumstances that formed the event, but the fact that this response seems possible and not outlandish indicates how deeply queer sexuality is imbricated with violence and murder toward queer people. As we witness Ennis' grisly and private speculation about how Jack died (which he can hardly share with Lureen), we encounter forms of pain that surround the suffering and demise of a queer man such as Jack.

The first form of such anguish is that it cannot be expressed. The narrative strands Ennis with his terrible thoughts which, at least by the film's conclusion, he continues to bear in solitude. Ennis' heroic solitude might appeal at some level as an emblem of further cowboy grit, but it also resonates with the sense of how queer deaths—especially after the advent of HIV, but also in terms of abiding forms of violence against queer women and men—have little public formal rite or notice.

If we frame this privating pain in the context of *Brokeback Mountain*'s historical dimension, we encounter the challenge of making sense of this solitude. Is it somehow nostalgic? Does it provoke us in the present era to consider how many LGBQT people in prior eras suffered such grief? Does it inadvertently give a strange comfort to us in that it suggests that somehow such solitary pain has been ameliorated or altered? Might we become too easily confirmed that such grief is not the case of how current forms of violence toward queer people abide in many settings?

How we answer these questions sheds light on the ways that we interpret the film's closing gesture. After having learned from Lureen that Jack's cremated remains will be divided, with part of them staying in Texas while the remainder of the ash is to be returned to Wyoming for scattering over Brokeback Mountain, we discover Ennis in his meeting with Jack's parents at the their home. Jack's father insists that his son's ashes will be placed in the local family plot and not on Brokeback Mountain, forming a final defiance of his son's wish.

Ennis is allowed to visit Jack's childhood bedroom, where he discovers hanging in the closet a memento that Jack has retained over the years: the shirts they were wearing on the final day of their first summer herding sheep in the mountains. That last day, we recall, the two men fought and their struggle brought blood; the blood stains remain on the two shirts that are now enfolded within each other. Ennis takes the shirts as the lone physical objects that retain the memory of their earliest encounter.

The film's concluding image leaves Ennis in his threadbare trailer as he, now home, retrieves the shirts from his own closet and remarks as he holds them, "Jack, I swear . . ." This cryptic comment, said to himself, forms the film's coda. What does Ennis swear to Jack? Typically, the speech-act of swearing is one of taking an oath, but an oath to do what? Recalling Jack's long-standing wish that the two of them might live and ranch together, Ennis' comment might offer at long last some commitment on Ennis' part to retain the memory of Jack that no one else might: as a man capable of intimacy and sexual vibrancy with another man. But, Ennis' oath, leaving off as it does with no specific act to which Ennis' will ally himself, can also suggest that he swears that he cannot make any sense of what has happened to him and to them. There are no words he can access that will finish the sentence.

Jane Tompkins comments about the Western that "[the] denial of sex being central to the kind of deprivation the Western finds essential for the exemplary life . . . the desert itself is the great exemplar of ascesis."[18] She continues that "there is something infinitely reassuring about this. Far from town, far from the conveniences of modern life, far from any outside help, the solitary man, with only nature at his disposal, makes himself comfortable."[19]

The description here has homologies with Ennis' final situation with the memory of Jack and with the bond that cannot be described, even to himself. Ennis may be safe—even if this home hardly seems to be a maternal one, but one that shelters the bloodied embracing shirts—but the conditions under which he can remain so demand silence of him.

Michel Foucault's last writings were themselves concerned with this idea of ascesis that Tompkins invokes. As he examined the writings in Greek and Roman culture that provided guidance about how one might conduct oneself ethically, he found the notion of a self-control which no one demands of an individual but which forms the basis for good conduct both toward oneself and toward others. Ascesis is not primarily about self-denial of one's pleasures, although it is often severe in its demands upon the man (and Foucault's account is about men) who practices it, but about understanding the limits of what is possible between what Foucault understood to be the dialectic of liberation and regulation as regards gender and sexuality.

While Foucault was writing about a historically past era, his interest in ascesis aligns with his pursuit of a different mode of thinking about sexuality that could invent, in the face of discipline by others, its own moral code. This code was the product of self-discipline and denial that might lead one to the good life; Foucault writes about it that "the object of this two-fold training was both to enable the individual to face privations without suffering, as they occurred, and to reduce every pleasure to nothing more than the elementary satisfaction of needs."[20] Within this sense of how one might conduct oneself, we might ask if Tompkins' invocation of ascesis within the Western that is *Brokeback Mountain* sheds light on Ennis del Mar's predicament at the film's conclusion. Within the terms that Foucault offers about the ascetic practice, Ennis is protected from assault on the memory of Jack Twist because he does not suffer but enjoys the memory of what has passed.

The student of queer theory might take this lesson to heart not solely as an invocation to understand how queer sexuality is a source of pleasure—for it is that, for why else would anyone seek it?—but is also a source of challenge, even in the present moment. And, this is not to discount the remarkable changes and the progress that LGBQT politics have wrought for many in the political and social domains of contemporary life. But it does remind us that the ability of queer life and queer theory to shape and renew life seems always to bring its own perils— perils that must be lived with and, too often, died with.

We should be wary of interpreting any narrative's conclusion as the sole manner in which we interpret the foregoing events in it, and a friend once told me that he fantasized that Ennis would continue on and find another boyfriend for himself. This galvanizing revelation, which is hardly supported by anything we witness in *Brokeback Mountain*, reminds us that we can take from narratives what we need in order to make sense of the world. As queer theory has reshaped our critical knowledge of how gender and sexuality, as well as race, ethnicity, and nationality as well, make us who we are, it remains vital for us to hope that its insights provide the opportunity for us to alter the anti-queer social world we inhabit. There are important lessons to be taken from Ang Lee's *Brokeback Mountain* as it allows us to perceive our assumptions about the meaning of same-sex sexuality and gendering within our lives; we can share Ennis' marring grief, his ascetic self-discipline, his memories of erotic joy, and we can also speculate about the world that begins at the film's conclusion.

Notes

1 Brenda Cooper and Edward C. Pease, "Framing Brokeback Mountain: How the Popular Press Corralled the 'Gay Cowboy Movie,'" *Critical Studies in Media Communication*, 25.3 (August 2008), 249.

2 Cooper and Pease, "Framing Brokeback Mountain," 258.

3 Christopher Lloyd, "Taboo Passion on the Range," Indianapolis Star, December 28, 2005. Quoted in Cooper and Pease, p. 259.

4 Cooper and Pease, "Framing Brokeback Mountain," 259–60.

5 Chris Berry, "The Chinese Side of the Mountain," *Film Quarterly*, 60.3 (Spring 2007), 33.

6 Berry, "The Chinese Side of the Mountain," 35.

7 Eve Kosofsky Sedgwick, *Touching Feeling: Affect, Pedagogy, Performativity* (Durham: Duke University Press, 2003), 149.

8 "Tongzhi" in this account translates roughly as any sexual minority.

9 William F. Schroeder, "On Cowboys and Aliens: Affective History and Queer Becoming in Contemporary China," *GLQ: A Journal of Lesbian and Gay Studies*, 18.4 (2012), 429.

10 Leslie Fiedler, "Come Back to the Raft Ag'in, Huck Honey," *Partisan Review*, June (1948), 721–48.

11 Jane Tompkins, *West of Everything: The Inner Life of Westerns* (New York: Oxford University Press, 1992), 71.

12 Tompkins, *West of Everything*, 81.

13 Ibid., 86.

14 Ed Buscombe, "Inventing Monument Valley: Nineteenth Century Landscape Photography and the Western Film," in *The Western Reader*, ed. Jim Kitses and Gregg Rickman (New York: Limelight Editions, 1998), 116.

15 Andre Bazin, "The Evolution of the Western," in *What Is Cinema? Volume 2*, trans. Hugh Gray (Berkeley: University of California Press, 1971), 151.

16 Buscombe, "Inventing Monument Valley," 118.

17 Ibid., 116.

18 Tompkins, *West of Everything*, 84.

19 Ibid., 81.

20 Michel Foucault, *The Use of Pleasure: Volume Two of the History of Sexuality*, trans. Robert Hurley (New York: Vintage Books, 1985), 73.

Conclusion

The historical dimensions of queer theory have meant for the field that it is both concerned with the past and engaged with the every-renewing present moment. Queer theory's activities of examining prior-going discourses, representations, and practices of gender and sexuality situate queer theorists with the legacy of what has gone before, and the field in its best iterations sees the past as shaping the present. How we conceive of what has led us to our current situations discloses to us the ideas that we inherit, often without perhaps even being aware of such. The project of challenging and dismantling forms of domination that either explicitly or tacitly aid or endorse exclusion, violence, and discrimination against LGBQT people is in part about seeing how received ideas about gender and sexuality can first be identified and second be demanded to account for themselves. Thus, queer theory relies upon understanding the historical past while living within the present.

This duality has important implications for scholars of film because cinema is an ever-expanding mode of cultural production, and the fact that a decade has passed since the release of *Brokeback Mountain* means that it, too, is a historical document, and one whose lessons reach back to the past of the 1960s to the 1980s, as well as the year 2005, as well the years since the film's first moments of circulation. Indeed, viewers new to the film may have their own assumptions about gender and sexuality shaped by the politics of LGBQT scholarship and activism since the film's appearance, making its project one that demands a historical accounting.

That said, a remarkable aspect of Lee's film is that no subsequent large-scale feature film has motivated the debates over queer sexuality that *Brokeback Mountain* did (and continues to do), a phenomenon that should make us wonder about the role that film plays in the cultural and political arenas of sexuality and gender. While there have certainly been important films about LGBQT life that have appeared, the reluctance on the part of the film industry, at least within the United States, to produce films that sponsor discussion of how gender and sexuality figure within our lives should make us wonder at the challenges of making cinema by and for queer people and their allies.

This marked absence of widely released queer-inflected Hollywood cinema highlights the long-standing conservatism within the film industry to underwrite films that might not seem to garner audiences beyond a niche of viewers interested in nonnormative gender and sexuality, a legacy that extends at least back to the 1930s, with the appearance of the Hollywood Production Code. (But, the emphasis here should be placed upon the fact that normative heterosexual sexuality drives much of the content of current film.) Other forces are at work as well, not least the fact that television, which now encompasses broadcast, cable, and live-streaming platforms for distribution, has been able to cater to those "niche" audiences in more nimble fashion than cinema has. Television, however, is hardly a less cost-intensive endeavor and brings with it other constraints, not least that viewers have an immense variety of options as to what they might view and how they might access content available through cable, satellite, plug-in apps such as Hulu and HBO Now, and web-based streaming interfaces such as Youtube and Vimeo.

These new options for the production and reception of moving-image content heralds a new moment in cinema, and one we can eagerly approach with the organizing ideas of queer theory. For example, the 2015 release directed by Sean S. Baker, *Tangerine*, was shot on iPhones and edited using desktop computer software. The film is a significant achievement formally and aesthetically and its narrative about African American trans sex-workers in contemporary Los

Angeles is one that might not have found funding were its costs typical of the production methods for most dominant corporate filmmaking. The relation between its relative inexpensiveness to manufacture and the topic with which it engages is perhaps no coincidence, making an argument for the possibility of new modes of image production made accessible through developing technologies of smart phones and image-handling software.

This relation between the economic and the cultural within queer cultural production is a long-standing and remarkable aspect of film, and one name for this has been camp. Camp more generally connotes a playful emphasis on style and has historically been thought to be a mode of cultural production and consumption among gay male subcultures prior to the advent of post-Stonewall identity politics. The governing techniques of camp are those that have allowed queer men in homophobic environments to shape the cultural product with both stylistic excess and with ambiguous codings of same-sex relations, marking them as acceptably homosocial for "straight" audiences all the while that camp productions often rely upon in-jokes to convey to sympathetic audiences that all is not what it appears. Concurrently, camp has been also understood as a form of reception of the cultural text, where the camp aesthetic shapes readings of films, novels, music, etc., by focusing upon the unanticipated forms of stylistic excess which appear in a text.

Drag performance forms one example of how this works. Drag, in which performers (often men) dress in the trappings of femininity, has often been seen as a vexing aspect of gender performance because of its capacity to seem degrading to women or to be unaware of its reliance upon stereotypes. This remains a strong response to drag only if we insist upon the notion of gender as essential or inherent. If gender performance is indeed that—a performance—then drag opens up new interpretive possibilities, where drag's fascination with feminine style as over-the-top redirects its critical impulses from women to the larger enterprise of gender conformity.

Highlighting as it so often does the fact of gender performance *as labor*, and femininity as particularly demanding, drag makes explicit the work of being gendered.

Only until recently has drag functioned within the sphere of cultural production more properly (although it was a practice associated with straight male comic performers such as Milton Berle in early US broadcast television). We can consider the recent television productions of *Rupaul's Drag Race* as a popularizer of the practice for audiences who may have few other opportunities to encounter drag beyond their television screens. But drag forms only one instance in which to consider how camp sensibilities have shaped recent film or television (and it might be distinctly instructive to read the performances of the male actors in *Brokeback Mountain* as "cowboy drag.")

It is hardly a coincidence that both Eve Sedgwick and Judith Butler each have written about camp and drag as important forms of queer critique because they question many of most cherished assumptions we might make about the naturalization of gender and sexuality, about the value of those cultural productions which do so, and they do so by considering this form of queer textual play as antagonizing dominant forms of heteronormative culture.[1] Within the study of film, scholarly literature on camp has developed its own medium-specific critical languages for making sense of camp codings within films as well as the practices of camp audiences who produce their own pleasures in response to films and television which may have not have been intended to be read as such.

This latter point brings us to a central part of queer theory as it relates to the study of culture: how queer readings of texts and performances alter our sense of the meaning of the commodified culture that surrounds us. The field of cultural studies, which began in the United Kingdom in the 1960s and has become a central field of inquiry around the world within the humanities and social sciences, has shaped much of the work on popular culture by queer theorists because cultural studies discerned the phenomenon of social subcultures as vital for the ways that we each, individually and collectively, engage with the cultural products which we encounter.

The fact that our culture so frequently takes the shape of products—of objects of economic exchange for the extraction of monetary profit—is a recent phenomenon of human societies, appearing only in the last few centuries under the expansion of capitalism as the dominant economic mode for human life. The practice of consuming a text that someone else—usually, a corporation—has manufactured on a mass basis for purchase is, within the scale of human history, the exception rather than the norm, and research in cultural studies makes a point of asking how we import cultural commodities into our lives in order to derive meaning from them.

A key insight of scholars in cultural studies that has shaped queer theory's research is the idea of the subculture, where subcultures form smaller groups of consumers whose tastes and interests foster social cohesion within the larger society and whose consumption of specific kinds of cultural commodities allows them to invent for themselves new interpretations of a given commodity. Music subcultures within the United Kingdom were among the first subcultures whose practices gave evidence that consumers, and especially younger consumers, were shaping their worlds through their musical tastes. The fact that these women and men, often adolescent, were working class and the fact that the post–Second World War expansion of the economy within the United Kingdom was making new consumer goods available provided the opportunity for music subcultures to embrace style—in clothing and fashion, hair and cosmetics, in product design, in dance, in slang and language usage, and in music production—to amalgamate the array of consumer goods in highly personalized and innovative ways. This combination and recombination of consumer objects was not "mere" consumerism, but was the expression of solidarity among people who were excluded from social privilege accorded to the middle and upper classes. While subcultural practices may not have always directly articulated subcultural style as a form of class consciousness or a nascent feminism, they often did express fantasies of liberation and freedom from the drudgery of everyday life and of labor in industrial societies.

The similarity of subcultural practices as described and theorized by cultural studies scholars regarding how queer people engage with the homophobic culture they live within has provided scholars of culture within queer theory— including those studying film and related media—with the means to identify how queer cultures are in point of fact queer *sub*cultures, "sub" both in the sense that they are contained within the larger matrix of society and in the sense that they are subordinate to many of its dominant assumptions and practices. A key problem for examining queer subcultures within the terms offered by cultural studies, though, has been that queer people are often at pains never to disclose their sexuality and their ostensible gender "deviance," and the things that they do with cultural products—the work of consumption, so to speak—often has demanded that they conceal their very presence as cultural consumers.

This need to dissemble by queers presents significant challenges for understanding within queer theory and queer studies the cultural practices that adhere to the way that queer men and women think about the films that they watch. This challenge is all the more intensified by the relative absence of films (and television) that depict the experience of being queer in terms other than those marked by stereotypes, homophobia, and anti-queer thinking. One way of understanding this tendency would be to consider the absence of a queer cinema in the current moment as the result of the normalization of queers within the popular culture, but this is probably being too generous. The New Queer Cinema of the 1990s stemmed from the sense of urgency in there needing to be a cultural practice that engaged and reflected the crises of queer life (HIV, anti-gay/lesbian legislation and regulation), and no one would currently make the case that the urgent questions of activism which sustained queer theory have disappeared from the present moment, although, like all problems of politics, the terms have inevitably changed.

One way in which the terms of queer politics and queer theory have shifted is that we now live in a public culture that is able to represent the fact of there being LGBQT people in the world without immediately resorting to defaming them. This is a small start toward the project of justice which queer theory labors to achieve. But, the presence of queer people within the popular culture—consider Ellen DeGeneres, Neil Patrick Harris, Wanda Sykes, or Laverne Cox, to name a handful—means more to the culture of celebrity than it does to the cinema, although the two are intertwined and have been for a long time. Yet, to be famous and queer does not necessarily ensure access to the processes through which cinema is manufactured; rather, it gives access to the machinery through which celebrity media is manufactured and, on some occasions, access in the former might be parlayed to opportunity in the latter. The recent cinema offers dismally few cases in which such has been the case.

We can, however, learn again from queer theory's questions about how this strange barrier between celebrity culture and film production works. It is a question of the biopolitics of the contemporary mediascape we inhabit. Foucault described various agents whose sexuality he understood to be emblems that the institutions of modern life—the state, corporations, medicine, the law, etc.—saw themselves as charged with regulating. The heterosexual couple, the child, the homosexual each became, for Foucault, a name of an aspect of sexuality which, within the matrices of power, needed to be overseen in order for the economic and national cultures to flourish.

Celebrity culture has developed in a similar fashion, with its repeated fascination with the bodies of young men and women, its coy languages about sexuality, and its reliance upon the motif of the scandal to draw readers' attention back to the apparently infinite demand for reportage about illicit sexualities. The impact of these new social agents as they are wielded by the media corporations, be they Gawker,[2] Facebook's news feed or, increasingly, *The New York Times* and *The Guardian*, is in inventing new agents of biopolitics; in the current moment, though, this occurs with less urgency of reproduction for national goals—the nineteenth-century ideal—and toward the production of consumption of celebrity news the appetite for which is apparently never sated.

The link between this development in tabloid reportage and the film industry's unwillingness to offer films that take seriously the lives of LGBQT people is a vital one because, without the scandal that might promote viewership of films like *Brokeback Mountain* and foster commentary upon them, filmmakers may produce smaller budgeted and vitally necessary films about queer life which sponsor little dialogue among audiences while the news culture endlessly seems to rediscover ostensible "perversion" among celebrities who in fact seldom appear in cinema.

Baker's film, *Tangerine*, though, marks an important turn, employing as it does nonbrand talent, using mobile low-cost production technologies and relying upon word-of-mouth endorsement in order to bring viewers to it through online portals. This may not be cinema in its most typical configurations, and that is the point of what queer theory has emphasized about the ongoing problem of LGBQT genders and sexuality for the field of representation that includes cinema.

In this regard, the intellectual and activist work of queer theory discovers new areas of inquiry, and it is met by the work of filmmakers whose labors are a form of queer theory as well, an effect of the transformation of the larger discourse by the work of queer intellectuals. The ways in which we think about gender and sexuality through the terms that queer theory has developed now reshape the sphere of cultural production if only because it now becomes possible for queer life to be represented as life-giving and worthy of respect.

Notes

1 See Eve Kosofsky Sedgwick, "Divinity: A Dossier, A Performance Piece, A Little Understood Emotion (written with Michael Moon)," in *Tendencies* (Durham: Duke University Press, 1993), 215–51 and Judith Butler, "Bodily Inscriptions, Performative Subversions," in *Gender Trouble* (New York: Routledge, 1999), 163–80.

2 On August 22, 2016, gawker.com and its websites were shut down.

FURTHER READING

Judith Butler, *Bodies That Matter: On the Discursive Limits of Sex* (New York: Routledge, 2011).

Butler expands upon the claims of performance theory made in *Gender Trouble* by arguing that the dominant languages about sexuality and gender which we employ and limit the ideas we have about how bodies are named and described within contemporary gender politics.

Steven Cohan, *Masked Men: Masculinity and the Movies in the Fifties* (Bloomington: University of Indiana, 1997).

The 1950s were important years of change within both the US corporate film industry and within popular ideas about gender and sexuality. Cohan examines changing norms of masculinity within films of the period as such new forms of gender performance hinted at queer sexualities.

Alexander Doty, *Making Things Perfectly Queer: Interpreting Mass Culture* (Minneapolis: University of Minnesota Press, 1993).

Doty was one of the first queer media theorists to argue that the ways that we discuss the making and viewing of cinema limit our ability to understand the ways that queers shape their interpretation of film and popular culture.

Richard Dyer, *The Culture of Queers* (London: Routledge, 2001).

Dyer's role in fostering queer critical media scholarship makes him a key thinker for students of film and contemporary culture. His multiple books on the subject of queers and film are all important reading and this volume is an excellent start.

Lee Edelman, *No Future: Queer Theory and the Death Drive* (Durham: Duke University Press, 2004).

Edelman critiques contemporary anti-queer politics through the figure of the child by examining literary and cinematic texts that pose the figures of queer people as inherently pernicious to the social order which ostensibly seeks to protect children and, by proxy, the future of human societies.

Michel Foucault, *Discipline and Punish: The Birth of the Prison* (New York: Vintage Books, 1995).

Appearing before *The History of Sexuality*, this book provides an expansive understanding of how Foucault understood the normalization of power in contemporary institutions. The history of prisons and penitentiaries offered here argues that the techniques of power and domination which Foucault developed subsequently were already at work in the reorganization of criminal law and prison design in the nineteenth century.

Ellis Hanson, ed., *Outtakes: Essays on Queer Theory and Film* (Durham: Duke University Press, 1999).

This collection of essays by different authors provides an array of queer theoretical approaches to the interpretation of film. The authors examine Hollywood and avant-garde films in order to understand how queer producers and consumers of film have created their own meanings of cinema.

Kara Keeling, *The Witch's Flight: The Cinematic, the Black Femme, and the Image of Common Sense* (Durham: Duke University Press, 2007).

The role of film in black liberation movements has been underestimated and misunderstood and Keeling argues that we need new historical and theoretical tools to understand the racism, homophobia, and misogyny at work in our visual culture.

José Esteban Muñoz, *Disidentifications: Queers of Color and the Performance of Politics* (Minneapolis: University of Minnesota Press, 1999).

Muñoz argues that queer people of color have forged their own intellectual and artistic technique for engaging with dominant (including queer) marginalization of ethnic and racial minorities.

Amy Villarejo, *Lesbian Rule: Cultural Criticism and the Value of Desire* (Durham: Duke University Press, 2003).

The specter of the lesbian as both cinematic image and as film spectator organizes Villarejo's account of Hollywood film, television, and video in a queer theoretical account that engages Marxist and Derridean modes of knowledge production.

Patricia White, *Uninvited: Classical Hollywood Cinema and Lesbian Representability* (Bloomington: Indiana University Press, 1999).

The Hollywood Production Code's prohibition of representation of "perverse" sexualities included that of the lesbian, and White offers a historical reading of films that suggested lesbian desire and sexuality.

INDEX